THE FIRST STEPS

A PARENT'S GUIDE TO FIGHTING AUTISM

Brad & Alisha Crawford

xulon PRESS

This book is dedicated to our son Brodie.

We are so proud of you and amazed at your perspective on life. You are an inspiration to your family and everyone blessed enough to meet you. We thank God for giving us such a wonderful son.

Brodie, at age 2 years 8 months, about 15 months into his therapy program.

Acknowledgements

Our Family & Friends

We are incredibly thankful for our families who have been there with us from the very beginning of our journey through autism. They have offered love, prayers, support, encouragement and active involvement in each and every step along the way. We always knew we had our families standing right beside us through the highs and lows, and we felt sustained by their prayers. We could never adequately thank each of them, but the special interest they all took in Brodie was something that we'll always treasure with gratitude in our hearts. Many times they gave us rest, spent extra time with Brodie, or simply served as a* *sounding board as we sought God's wisdom for the next step. There are not enough words to tell you how much you've blessed us.*

Brodie's Therapists, Doctors, & Teachers

We also want to extend a big thank you to the many professionals who have assisted us along the way. Brodie would be nowhere near where he is today without them and their willingness to share their wisdom. Thank you to: Sue Kline, who helped move us through the system early on; Nancy Levos, who was our first speech therapist and was an angel who gave us hope and so many practical ways of helping Brodie right from the start; Dawn, Anne and Bunny, who were also a great help with Brodie in that first year; Stevie, who was always so energetic and positive, and who taught Brodie his first word – you are a great friend and will always hold a special place in our hearts for all you've done for our family; Darcy, who spent endless hours counseling and problem-solving with us; Dolores, who provided a wealth of wisdom and many great ideas; Misten, who stepped in and provided struc-

ture and stability to Brodie's team and helped Alisha brainstorm through many different stages of Brodie's development.

We have many therapists, consultants and teachers to thank as well, who all played important roles in Brodie's development. Thank you to: Lisa, Janet, Molly, Christina, Beth, Connie, Suzy, Pam and Suzie; who worked tirelessly each day to ensure that Brodie was reaching his full potential. Thank you to: Mrs. Mayfield, Teacher Jolene, Mrs. Robino, Dr. Meager, Mrs. Muller, Mrs. Greenstone, Miss Jenn, Miss Kim, and Mrs. Staff; the many teachers who poured their time and efforts into helping Brodie navigate his way through pre-K, Kindergarten, and first grade with success, hard work, and fun. Thank you to: Kathy Carraway, who is not only our beloved friend and neighbor, but also served as Brodie's part-time aide in Kindergarten and has been a wonderful mentor and encouragement to our family. Thank you to: Dr. John Green in Oregon City, Oregon, who has been a great source of knowledge and the brains behind our successes in strengthening and stabilizing Brodie's digestive system.

God has answered our prayers many times over the years by placing very special and talented people in Brodie's life who truly loved him, and saw him not only for who he was on the inside, but also for what he could become. We know that many days were harder than others, and in those times, we saw your drive and determination to see that Brodie pulled through. What you have done for him will not be forgotten.

Table of Contents

CHAPTER 2 –

INTRODUCTION

A Parents' Perspective

*O*ur son, Brodie, has led our family on an incredible journey over the past few years. He has changed our lives in so many ways: our outlook on life and our sense of what's important. We knew next to nothing about autism before Brodie, but after embarking on a real-life crash course, battling and overcoming autism has become one of the main focal points of our life.

We wrote this book not as licensed professionals or certified academics, but rather, as parents who have endured and are enduring this battle. There are many professionals, experts and even parents who are more knowledgeable than we are on any of the topics discussed in this book. What we've tried to do is to simply compile the most critical information you need at the start of your journey to proceed rapidly.

A Quick Guide to the Basics

Though our book targets parents or primary care-givers of children with autism, the principles and infor-mation we've assembled will benefit almost anyone who is impacted by the disorder. The aim of this book is to give you a brief tour through the complicated world of autism treatment so that you will be equipped to seek out the most well-rounded treatment program to help your child or loved one as quickly as possible. It is in no way a comprehensive book on the subject of autism and therefore will not go nearly as in-depth as the topic warrants.

Scope & Resources

Throughout the book and also in Appendix B, we've included several resources on a variety of subjects related to autism to help you further investigate partic-ular areas of concern for your child. Many books have *been written on most every aspect of autism, and we will share some of these titles to help you get started in the right direction.*

Equipping for Success

One frustration we had early on in our journey was that most of the books we came across were devoted to sharing the accounts of one child's story with helpful information scattered throughout. For us, we wanted to learn as much as we could as quickly as possible so that we could get busy helping Brodie. So, we ended up reading, and at times skimming, several books to piece together the important information we needed on diet, biomedical intervention, therapies, and other helpful techniques. In this book, we've tried to touch on each of these briefly so you can get busy helping your child.

Writing this book is also a way for us to share what we've learned in hopes of helping other parents enjoy some of the same victories we've experienced. **Our goal is to first equip you with a positive and empowered outlook, and second, to offer a practical guide for helping your child.** *The chapters in this book are* structured so that you can quickly implement the tools we wished we had at the onset of our own journey – that is, some strategies you can employ to help your child even before formal therapy begins.

Recipes

We have included a number of recipes in Appendix A at the back of the book that may help you meet your loved one's special dietary needs (see chapters 7 and 8 for more on this topic). These recipes have been developed by adding, subtracting, and substituting ingredients in that do not conflict with Brodie's special dietary needs. After many hours of trial and error, Alisha and our moms have landed on a variety of tasty food replacements for our family.

Encouragement & Hope

We understand the feeling of devastation and the perceived "death of dreams" that parents face when they discover autism is a part of their child's life. It's no wonder that so many remain in denial of what they're facing. But there is good news! These little ones have so much potential that there is great cause for hope.

And even better news – there IS something you can do to help that hope become a reality. Autism treatment has improved so much in recent years that the sky is the limit for some of these kids. Those dreams you may have written off now might be possible again. And while they may end up different from how you imagined, if we're honest, most of the times those dreams are more about us than they are our children. But that's another topic for another book!

It's very important that you maintain high hopes for your child's success, but it's also important that your hopes for them are not clouded by your own agenda. They may not be able to communicate it yet, but they definitely have their own thoughts, likes, dislikes, plans, goals, and dreams of their own. As their parent, it is your job to help support them so they may one day reach those goals and dreams. There's no doubt that it will take an above-average amount of effort on your part to help your special needs child. But that's our job as parents – to do whatever it takes to support and help our children succeed in life.

We wish you much success in your journey and our prayer is that your lives will be as blessed by your child as ours have been by Brodie.

Introducing our Family

Before you read on, we wanted to take the time to introduce ourselves. We are a family of five – Brad, Alisha, and our three sons, Brodie, 8, Jonah, 6, and Graysen, 5.

We currently live in Kampala, Uganda. We have been here for 2 years on a missions trip, where I serve as a structural engineer and East Africa office director for Engineering Ministries International, a non-profit Christian organization committed to bringing hope for people in developing nations. Alisha was a stay-at-home mom, but now that our boys are all in school she is back to teaching (Kindergarten) at the school the boys attend, Heritage International School. She spends most of her time mothering our boys, helping them with school work, and mentoring a local Ugandan teacher in her classroom. The boys love school, playing in the yard, riding bikes, swimming at the local American swim club, and playing soccer. Brodie also enjoys taking piano lessons from the music teacher at his school. We have three very busy, delightful boys who bring smiles and joy to our life each day, coupled of course, with a healthy dose of mischief!

Our Son's Diagnosis

Soon after we realized that Brodie was on the autism spectrum at age 17 months, he was given a medical diagnosis for autism from our pediatrician and therefore qualified for formal treatment through our local school district. Jonah and Graysen, who both showed immune system and dietary problems that were symptomatic of autism at an early age, are now typically developing, energetic boys. Both Jonah & Graysen also no longer have the food intolerances they battled early in life.

CHAPTER 1 –

A BASIC INTRODUCTION TO AUTISM

*W*e had been at a family reunion for four days when my sister Terri commented, "Hey, Brodie just looked up at me for the first time (on this visit)!" At the time, we didn't think a whole lot about it being first time parents. Brodie was 14 months old at the time, and we were well used to the fact that he had his own agenda and preferred to tackle it alone most of the time. But the comment hung in the back of our minds.

About a month later, Alisha was on the phone with her sister-in-law Shannon when the topic of Brodie came up. Alisha asked Shannon if her youngest at the time, Tyler, could understand a one-step command like,

"Go get your shoes" at age 15 months. "Oh yeah, he could do that" was the reply. "Wow, Brodie doesn't even understand what shoes are," was Alisha's thought. As she pieced Terri's comment from the family reunion together with this conversation, she knew we had a problem. This began a two-month search to figure out what that problem was.

About all we knew of autism before Brodie was what we had seen in the movie 'Rain Man' and Brodie was not like the Rain Man at all. What we didn't know was that the autism spectrum is wide and the range of symptoms all encompassing. As we discovered later, the Rain Man character is actually considered a savant, which is a relatively rare type of autism where the individual is extremely impaired in most areas, but has one or more striking, super-human abilities - such as the ability to play a musical instrument perfectly with no prior training, or the ability to solve very complex mathematical equations instantaneously, or in Rain Man's case, the photographic memory that allowed him to count cards in a poker game or a dropped box of toothpicks at just a glance.

What is Autism?

Autism Spectrum Disorder (ASD) is referred to as a 'spectrum' disorder because its range of characteristics is so wide. The spectrum is like a color wheel, where the number of colors is virtually infinite. In autism, every child's story is a different one, with a different combination of symptoms, behaviors, sensitivities, strengths and weaknesses.

Generically, the disorder is defined by its symptoms, as opposed to a measurable, physical manifestation. While certain digestive and gastrointestinal abnormalities seem to be fairly consistent amongst afflicted individuals, the more recognizable symptoms are typically described as affecting communicative, cognitive, social and imaginative abilities. There's a very accurate saying in the autism community: "If you've seen one child with autism, you've seen ONE child with autism!" This speaks to the fact that though there is a pool of common characteristics, no two cases on the spectrum are the same. Since at this time there are an estimated 1.0 to 1.5 million[1] Americans with autism, the challenges facing parents and therapists alike are staggering.

The Autism Spectrum

There are many different names and syndromes associated with the autism spectrum: Autism Spectrum Disorder or ASD, Pervasive Developmental Disorder (PDD), Pervasive Developmental Disorder – Not Otherwise Specified (PDD-NOS) (sometimes called Atypical Autism), Kanner's Syndrome, Asperger's Syndrome, and others. Many parents are mistakenly relieved when their child's doctor diagnoses their child using a different name on the spectrum, such as 'PDD'. Unfortunately, these parents soon learn that these other names all refer to the same autism spectrum of developmental disorders.

It's important to note that sometimes in common vernacular, a few of these other names may refer to milder cases of autism. For instance, Asperger's Syndrome is generally considered to be on the milder end of the autism spectrum. Oftentimes, children with Asperger's show little or no speech delay, and overall can be very high-functioning individuals.

Autism: When does it appear?

Autism can surface as either regressive or non-regressive. Children with regressive autism appear to develop typically up to age 36 months or even older, and then suddenly regress significantly in their speech, ability to comprehend language, and/or other areas of development. Children with non-regressive autism begin to show signs of developmental delays much earlier. Rather than losing their skills abruptly, as in regressive autism cases, they fail to demonstrate these skills by the appropriate age (ex. eye contact, engaging with others, babbling, waving, pointing, etc.). Our son Brodie's case was non-regressive.

You may have heard about the drastic increase in cases of autism over the past 10 to15 years. According to data from a 2002 study released in 2007 by the U.S. Centers for Disease Control and Prevention, the rate of autism in the U.S. is approximately 1 in 150 children – compared to 4 or 5 in 10,000 in recent decades (the study also reconfirmed the rate is 3 to 4 times higher in boys than in girls)[2]. These rising statistics are alarming, leading many in the autism community to conclude that some form of environmental toxin is playing a role in the increase of incidents (we'll discuss this in a little more detail later).

Symptoms of Autism

If you have not yet confirmed that your child has autism, there are many telltale signs to observe. Each of the signs can occur in typically developing children, so the appearance of one or a couple of the signs does not necessarily indicate autism. However, it is unusual for a typically developing child to display multiple items from this list.

In our case, when we first looked at the prospect of Brodie having autism, we went down the list checking almost every indicator. As I was driving home from a soccer game one night in October of 2002, Alisha read the list to me over the phone. I remember remarking something about how the list she was reading seemed to be a personalized description of our son!

There are many comprehensive lists of symptoms and early warning signs available online – www.autism.org has compiled a list of a number of these websites. Here is a sample of some of the more common indicators:

- *avoids eye contact with others*
- *doesn't smile or otherwise acknowledge familiar people*
- *exhibits delayed or disordered speech*
- *lacks non-verbal communication or gesturing (waving, pointing, clapping, etc.)*
- *lacks the ability to comprehend language (e.g. doesn't respond to his name, doesn't respond to simple requests)*
- *fails to imitate others' actions*
- *prefers being alone; doesn't interact with others in play activities*
- *doesn't play with toys in a manner consistent with their intended use*
- *fixates on moving or spinning objects*
- *lacks imaginative play skills (e.g. pretending to talk on the phone, etc.)*
- *reacts adversely to sensory stimulation (e.g. bright lights, loud noises, crowded rooms, etc.)*
- *exhibits repetitive or odd behaviors*
- *has noticeable, physical under or over-activity*
- *displays an inability to understand emotions*

- *demonstrates injurious behavior towards self/ others*
- *throws frequent tantrums for no apparent reason*
- *displays "splinter skills" (i.e. extremely gifted in some areas while severely delayed in others)*
- *suffers from frequent skin rashes, constipation or diarrhea*
- *is a very picky, even unusual, eater (many times, children with autism will only want to eat foods that are a certain color!)*
- *sleeps either too much or very little for his or her age*

What Autism is NOT

For decades, autism was lumped together with mental retardation. Because so little was known about the disorder, individuals with autism were often institutionalized for their entire lives. Fortunately, so much has been learned about autism over the past 30 years that this is no longer the case. The vast differences between autism and mental retardation are well understood now. In fact, many individuals with autism are extremely intelligent and do quite well in school. It's important for parents to understand that an autism diag-nosis is not a death sentence, nor is it an untreatable condition. Concerning the long term prospects for indi-viduals with autism, Stephen Edelson with the Center for the Study of Autism in Salem, Oregon, writes in his 'Overview of Autism':

"In contrast to 20 years ago, when many autistic individ-uals were institutionalized, there are now many flexible living arrangements. Usually only the most severe indi-viduals live in institutions. In adulthood, some people with autism live at home with their parents; some live in residential facilities; some live semi-independently (such as in a group home); and others live indepen-dently. There are autistic individuals who graduate from college, and receive graduate degrees; and some develop adult relationships and may marry."[3]

Causes and Cures

At this point, many experts feel that there is most likely no single cause for autism, but rather a number of factors, both genetic and environmental, that align to impact an individual's development. Many researchers

35

have focused recently on finding the 'autism gene'. However, there is speculation that multiple genes are likely associated with the disorder. While there is no known cure for autism, afflicted children can improve dramatically if they receive professional help and have dedicated and motivated parents. A significant increase in research has occurred over the past 15-20 years, and new information is coming in all the time.

Genetic Factors

Many experts believe that a genetic susceptibility is likely involved on some level, along with environmental and biological contaminations. The genetic tie may not even be traceable in some instances, lurking under the surface for generations. With Brodie, no other relatives appear to have any connection to autism going back at least 3 generations on both sides.

Environmental & Biological Triggers

One popular feeling in the autism community that is gaining momentum is that a genetically susceptible individual may encounter an environmental or biological "trigger" during gestation or early childhood. This would explain the fact that about half of afflicted children show signs very early on, while others appear to develop typically for 18 to 36 months before regressing into autism.[4] The most often mentioned suspected trigger is mercury-poisoning, which can be ingested through certain fish, injected into the individual through immunizations, or enter the individual in the womb through the mother's bloodstream (mother's are commonly given the MMR or flu shot during pregnancy). Some evidence suggests that virus' can cause autism. The rubella and cytolomegalo viruses, as well as measles (MMR) and pertussis (DPT) vaccinations, are all suspected by some to be somehow associated with autism.[5]

Mercury & Other Heavy Metals Poisoning

Some in the autism community believe that the disorder is actually just mercury poisoning occurring in people with a genetically impaired ability to excrete heavy metals from their system. Whether or not this theory proves true, eliminating exposure to, and possibly even removing, any heavy metals that may be contaminating your autistic child seems to play an important role in getting him/her on the road to recovery. Other heavy metals that may surface through testing of children with autism include dangerously high amounts of lead, tin, aluminum, and others. And, while finding the cause of autism is critical to stopping the exploding rate of occurrence, finding effective ways to treat and overcome the disorder is an equally important undertaking for the thousands of families already impacted by it.

The Immune System & Gastrointestinal Issues

The close ties some doctors are finding between autism, the immune system, and the gastrointestinal tract is one of the newer areas of autism treatment research. Some of the most exciting breakthroughs are occurring in this field, as children are responding dramatically to dietary and biochemical interventions. This is why we place a heavy emphasis in this book on finding and rigidly sticking to a highly specialized diet tailored to your child. It's one of the more difficult aspects of the lifestyle change you'll be making, but also one of the most rewarding.

Is There Hope?

Perhaps the most common question among parents of children with autism when they first learn of their child's condition is: "Is this a lifelong sentence for my child?" As stated above, there is no known cure or 'magic pill'. However, the best case scenario for some children with autism is to make what is termed as a 'full recovery'. Generally, this means that the individual is able to overcome his condition and function in a typical environment with only residual autistic characteristics.

The term cure is not used because there's no real evidence that individuals biologically get rid of their autism. However, some individuals with autism can be indistinguishable from their peers and may live typical lives. While each child has their own level of potential, the goal of each parent should be for their child to reach his or her maximum potential, whatever that may be.

The First Thing to Do – Don't Wait to Get Help!

The single most important factor in your child's chances for success in fighting autism is time. The younger an affected child starts receiving substantial help, the higher the chances for recovery are and the more opportunities there are for the most comprehensive recovery possible. Far too many parents play the wait and see game, wasting extremely valuable time in hopes that the problem will go away. Instead, we encourage you to get busy at working to make the problem go away!

If you see a pattern of these indicators in your child, you should contact your pediatrician promptly. In the next chapter, we explain how we sought professional help.

CHAPTER 2 –

SEEK PROFESSIONAL EVALUATION & TREATMENT

*S*eeking professional help may not be as straight-forward as it sounds. Who do you call? Are there specialists in the medical field who should evaluate your son or daughter? Should you contact a private organization to receive therapy? The answers to these questions can be difficult to sort through, and they may in fact vary from place to place.

In general, most public autism services are handled through the local school district, and include speech therapy, occupational therapy, behavioral therapy and autism consultants (who coordinate the child's *individualized program with the parents). But quali-fying for these services may take you on a long and twisting road through your healthcare provider. In our town, individuals must first receive a referral from their primary care physician. Once the referral is made, the local school district will do another evaluation to qualify the student for educational services. So it is possible for a child to receive a medical diagnosis for autism, but still not qualify for educational services if the school district's team of specialists determine that the child does not require special assistance. Many states and even cities may be different in how they handle the evaluation process, but regardless, it is important for parents to be very proactive from the start.*

TAKE ACTION

Many parents don't seek professional help until long after they first start suspecting autism. But even if parents seek an evaluation for autism quickly, there can still be a substantial delay before the child is actu-ally evaluated. It is not uncommon to be given an eval-uation date three or more months away, depending on where you live. Evaluation specialists may even tell

---

you that it is important to observe children closely and document their behavior for up to four months before attempting to diagnose them with a disability.

Whichever the case, the time lost during this waiting period can be costly. Research has shown that the earlier you intervene in your child's development, the greater the long-term potential for his or her recovery.[6] It is therefore crucial that parents find a way to first minimize the length of the delay as much as possible, and second, make good use of the time while they are waiting. See Chapter 5 on how to start helping your child immediately.

Be a 'Squeaky Wheel'

But the first thing to do is to make an appointment with your child's primary care physician to start the evaluation process, and perhaps contact the local school district to learn how autism services are handled. From the standpoint of helping your child, however, this is precious time that just cannot be wasted by sitting idly on a waiting list. By calling regularly to check for cancellations and essentially becoming the 'squeaky wheel', you may be able to move up your evaluation date significantly, particularly since human nature will tend to make anyone want to help someone who shows an active, educated interest in being proactive. If this still doesn't get you in sooner, look into having your child evaluated outside your immediate area.

Be Positive

We should pause to mention at this point that being a squeaky wheel does not mean complaining. Quite the opposite, actually. We have run across so many parents who, in their desperation, forget the old adage, "You catch more flies with honey than with vinegar." From the beginning, we decided that no matter how tough our situation got, we would remain calm and friendly with the people we were working with. We realized that we were a direct reflection on Brodie, and any ill-feelings that developed against us would certainly affect how Brodie was treated. Beyond that, it really reduces your own stress to uplift people rather than demonize them.

Also, in many instances the people we dealt with were simply following the guidelines set by someone above them and had little to do with the final deci-

sion. *Barking at the middle-man is generally ineffective. Over and again, in the face of a difficult situation at one of his meetings, we would just calmly reiterate our desire to do what was best for Brodie. Somehow that just always seemed to redirect the conversation towards a solution.*

Put Your Child's Best Foot Forward

Another thing we did to try to give Brodie every advantage (whether during the evaluations or therapy sessions once he was placed in the program) was to make sure that he was always clean, his hair was combed (though Brodie hated having his hair combed) and he was dressed nicely. All of these little things may seem insignificant, but they can make a big difference in how your little child is perceived and even treated. It's not a bad thing if you can tug a little on the heart-strings of the therapists.

CHAPTER 3 –

START A JOURNAL

The Importance of Journaling

*I*f you decide to take action, even before having your child evaluated by professionals, one thing that is absolutely necessary is that you take careful notes of your child's progress. Keep weekly or even daily notes of significant things your child learns or still struggles with. This may be important once you finally meet with therapists so they are aware of where your child started if he or she begins improving from your initial efforts. If you don't keep track of your child's progress, you may risk disqualifying or delaying your child from receiving services due to the improvements you've made prior to the evaluation.

Help Identify Patterns & Problems

For our family, the process of becoming an expert on Brodie included starting a journal tracking Brodie's behavior patterns. Keeping a brief, up to date log of how he did each day allowed us to quickly zero in on his problem areas as well as his strengths. It later became a valuable tool for the therapists as well, as they were able to compare with their own notes to see how Brodie was doing in different developmental areas across multiple settings (e.g. school and home).

From the beginning, Alisha took a few minutes each night to rate Brodie's eye contact on a scale of 1 to 5 in a journal, as well as jot down any behavior changes we saw that day (e.g. not sleeping through the night). In time, we became accustomed to the habit of evaluating Brodie's actions throughout the day, which in turn helped us notice patterns of behavior that indicated a deficit or strength for Brodie. You will find a sample of Brodie's behavior, food, sleep, and stool charts included in Appendix C.

Record Breakthroughs and Progress

The tricky part is recognizing the small stuff. By sharing these little accomplishments with family and friends, you'll find it easier to maintain a positive outlook, and also to see the fruits of your labor. This is one thing Alisha was very good at - spotting the little steps forward. The following is an excerpt from Brodie's journal dated January 6, 2003:

"Today, I taught Brodie how to brush my hair. Later that day, he walked over and took a different brush out of the drawer and started to comb his own hair. It was exciting that he generalized this concept to a different brush and to his own hair."

For a typical child, this might seem insignificant. Yet for a child with autism, learning to generalize brushing hair, from mom's hair to his own was a significant step for Brodie at that stage of development.

CHAPTER 4 –

GET YOUR ATTITUDE RIGHT

Facing the Facts

*W*hen we first discovered that autism would be a part of Brodie's life on the evening of October 15th, 2002, we were full of a thousand emotions. We were stunned at the realization of such a major event happening in our lives. Yet, we were also partially relieved to finally understand what was going on with our son. It was sad to think of what opportunities or experiences he might have to miss out on later in life, and also a little scary to contemplate how our lives would have to change and may never be what we had 'dreamed' they'd be up to that point.

The day after we found out about Brodie, we kept cycling through all these different emotions. We asked God to not let it be true, that somehow we were just mistaken. Though back then I was seldom moved to tears, that evening after work I remember coming home and sobbing in the closet as I changed out of my work clothes. It was the first time I fully allowed myself to come to grips with what was happening. Little did I know that on the opposite end of the house, at the same time, Alisha was doing the same thing! To that point, we had both tried to stay strong for the other person. Finally, the gravity of the situation overwhelmed us.

Fortunately, there was also a God-given element of competitiveness in us. Somewhere down deep was a mindset that we could do and handle anything with God's help and do whatever it took for Brodie to succeed in life.

Acceptance

Shortly after that lone crying spell, however, a switch seemed to flip in both of us. Suddenly, we both felt this feeling of calmness and peace about the situation. It's hard to explain, but our perspective seemed to change almost instantly towards focusing on our plan of action and ignoring any thoughts of lost dreams for our son. Looking back, we feel this feeling was nothing that we accomplished on our own, but was a God-given answer to our family's prayers. God placed that feeling in each of our hearts, which in essence said, "This is my plan for you. You don't have time to pity yourselves. You need to get busy right away! This is not an accident, but something I have been preparing you for from the beginning. Remember, I won't give you anything that you can't handle, and I'll be at your side to help you through this." A number of scriptures we read during this time confirmed our feeling.

For me, as a chronic worrier, the total peace I felt was as foreign a feeling as I had ever had. Literally, once the tears stopped flowing, my attitude completely changed. To this day I can't explain, apart from the fervent prayers of our family, our ability to so quickly turn into a focused, forward-thinking team whose only concern was helping our son. We had no sense of fear, sorrow or regret for the massive fork in the road our lives had just taken – only committed determination.

Your Biggest Assets

Looking back on this transition time for us, I hope that if no other point gets across that readers will understand three things as they enter into the world of autism: 1) the importance of a positive and determined outlook; 2) prayer can have a powerful impact on your situation; 3) your biggest ally could be the support of your friends, family, or support group – so find some people who will join you in this journey.

Again, it bears repeating: it is essential that parents obtain and maintain a positive, can-do, never-give-up attitude. That cannot be overstated. Without it, everything from your marriage to the success of your child's recovery is at risk. It truly is the largest weapon in the arsenal a parent of autism has, and it literally can make or break your child's ability to reach his/her full potential. For us, this positive spirit was a blessing that came as a result of the prayers of our family and friends. We are forever grateful to them for interceding on our behalf, and to God for answering our prayers.

Your Worst Enemies

Denial is a killer when it comes to autism. Parents who refuse to accept the reality of the situation and opt to wait it out to see if the problems go away may be unwittingly lowering their child's potential as each day and hour passes. Early diagnosis and intervention are two of the most important factors in recovery. Far too many children are hindered by their parents' denial. The longer it takes for your child to start getting help, the further behind he/she will be.

Everyone struggles on some level with the mindset of "it could never happen to me", and unfortunately, autism all too often strikes the least likely and least suspecting people. In our case, neither of us could find any hint of autism or other developmental disorders in our family going back at least two or three generations. We had no inkling that this disorder may be lurking in our genes. In fact, we were very ignorant about autism as a whole. Yet somehow, with no hint, forewarning or telegraph, autism found its way into our family. Just believing that something so big was actually happening to us was in itself difficult to grasp.

Had we reacted differently at the beginning, refusing to accept what our gut was telling us, we're convinced Brodie would be nowhere near the thriving young boy he is today. There's little doubt that the son we know and love today would still be trapped in a confusing world of overwhelming sensory stimulations with far less ability to communicate with the outside world. Some children may be more difficult to diagnose, so acting decisively from the outset may be more challenging for some. But for others (this was the case with us), there is a point very early on when deep inside they notice that their child is a little different. Whether or not they are able to admit it is the difficult part. If you roll the dice and hope it goes away, you can cost yourself and your child lost time that is irretrievable. If, however, you act on your suspicions immediately, there really is nothing to lose, and you give your child the greatest possible chance for recovery. Even if your child does not have autism, getting them early help for learning or developmental disabilities will be beneficial to their progress.

Seeking Help Quickly

After our night of realization, Brad's sister gave us the phone number of a friend who has a son with autism. Their son had received help for a few years prior to that point and was now doing very well. We called her the next day and picked her brain about everything she had gone through with her son and asked her advice on how to get started. Soon after, we made an appointment for an evaluation with our pediatrician. But perhaps most importantly, on the advice of the friend, we started engaging Brodie as much as we could virtually every waking moment (we discuss how we did this in more detail later). We worried a little that the poor kid had no down-time, but we also knew he had a lot of catching up to do, and everything we were reading told us that the more interaction the better for these kids. We reasoned that although he might not have as easy and carefree a childhood as a typical kid would, without hard work early in life he would miss out on a lifetime of typical experiences.

By the time we went to the doctor's appointment 2 weeks later, we had spent so much time researching autism and Brodie's symptoms that we already had him diagnosed in our minds. Consequently, we spent most of the appointment convincing the doctor of what we were already certain of, noting each and every sign of autism he was showing. The doctor seemed taken aback by our matter of fact demeanor, but as we explained, our only focus was getting Brodie on the road to recovery as fast as possible.

There is hope

If you're really struggling with finding hope, take heart in the fact that children with autism have great potential to improve, and many times that potential is tremendous. It may help to think of your child as being trapped and needing your help to untangle the complicated web that binds him or her. What a gift it is to have the ability to help your child in such a tangible way! You will have to wage a complete physical, emotional and spiritual battle, but your efforts will be fruitful. Remember, every child has his own unique potential, ranging from somewhat limited to virtually unlimited. While everyone hopes for a full recovery, it's important to switch your focus from achieving a specific outcome to helping your child achieve his or her best.

We have mentioned prayer several times in this chapter, but we cannot overstate the importance of how it has helped us on a daily basis. Prayer has played a huge part in our approach to helping Brodie. We prayed for Brodie's progress, for our own stamina and perseverance, for wisdom, for our marriage, and for sleep! We had hundreds of family and friends praying for Brodie.

As different situations with Brodie's therapy arose, or when Brodie had a rough day, we'd email the family and let them know the specific prayer request. Time and again we were blessed by little 'miracles' that we attribute to Brodie being "covered in prayer" by our family, as Brodie would get the extra time we wanted for therapy, or out of the blue he would sleep through the night for the first time in months. Plus, the peace of mind derived from knowing that so many people were petitioning God on our behalf was an irreplaceable, stabilizing force in our lives.

Our Purpose in Life

There is no doubt that you will be challenged in this journey above and beyond what many people are able *to handle. Be reassured in your circumstance though, and realize you were chosen for this task because of your unique gifts and abilities. God isn't picking on you; rather, he's picking you to help one of his precious children overcome a huge obstacle in his or her life. What a calling! In fact, you may have even had the thought growing up that some big task lay ahead in your life. This was the case for both Alisha and I.*

Perhaps you weren't paying attention when you were younger, or you were distracted by your own plans for your life, but God has been preparing you for this your whole life. While no one, us included, feels prepared at the onset, the personality strengths and gifts that you have somewhere inside are well-suited for this calling, no matter how trivial they may seem.

Some examples of how we feel we were made to help Brodie:

- *Both of us are perfectionist, clean-freak types, which is perfect for Brodie who struggles with staying focused in chaotic settings.*
- *Alisha is a natural teacher (who taught 1st grade before having children).*

- *In many ways, I think a lot like Brodie, and there are a lot of similarities in our strengths and weaknesses. This has been helpful at times when we're brainstorming on how to teach Brodie certain things or helping him solve problems.*

- *Alisha is a very structured person and mom who almost always has a plan in place for the day, which is perfect for Brodie who thrives on a clearly defined schedule laid out before him (we've used visual schedules too, such as picture-strips or lists).*

- *As detail-oriented people (this is how "perfectionists" refer to themselves!), we can also very easily spot things that may bother Brodie ahead of time (who is an exacting perfectionist himself!) and either fix them before it throws him off, or better yet, walk him through the process of dealing with it – a dirty room, twisted socks in his shoes, taking a different route home in the car, toys that are missing parts, etc.*

- *We also have a number or sensory issues ourselves, so we are better equipped to recognize* and understand how Brodie is feeling about certain conditions or situations.

These are just a few of the ways in which our personalities, strengths and even weaknesses are perfectly suited for Brodie's needs. So whatever personality traits you have, there's little doubt that they will be valuable to the specific needs of your child – because you were made to take on this challenge! If you don't know your strengths, take time to list them out and periodically think about how you can focus them on helping your child. If you need help, ask your spouse, parents, family and friends what they see in you. This can be a healthy process not only for your child, but also for you!

When you have a chance to meditate sometime, think back over your life and recall some of those pivotal points, where a big decision or even a big mistake was made, or something happened to you that totally changed your life. In each case, your attitude and perspective probably played a large part in determining whether the outcome of the situation was positive or negative.

Our pastor often repeats the popular quote, "Your life is 10% what happens to you, and 90% how you react to it." Not to diminish the fact that bad things do happen, but very often the bad things turn out to carry blessings with them in the long run. With autism, this can and will be the case! If you have been given a child with autism, consider it your purpose for this chapter in life. Though much will be required of both you and your child, there are many blessings that await you as well.

The Blessings of Autism in Your Life

Having a child depend on you so much more than a typical child is very demanding, both physically and mentally, but it is also extremely rewarding when the breakthroughs come. As you begin your journey, your eyes will be opened to appreciate the small, oftentimes unnoticed things in life. We can remember the feelings of pure joy we felt when Brodie started looking us in the eyes, or when, after 3 months of therapy, he spoke his first word at age 22 months (the word was "Dah" which to him was "Go"). Since there are no guarantees for progress, we not only noticed but celebrated each and every step of forward progress he made. This is an important part of a parent's state of mind in this process since a positive attitude thrives when it is constantly being fed with little successes.

As we stated in the chapter on journaling, recognizing the small victories is so important. One family we know started a blog to chart and share their son's accomplishments. What a great way to keep family and friends up to date with your child's progress. Having an outlet for sharing will also help train you to look for the little steps of improvement.

Finding Balance & Time-off as Parents

Everyone needs balance in their life, so if you are not getting at least a small break every now and then you are heading down a dangerous road that could end in disaster. If you are married, each spouse should do their part to give their mate a break. Alisha was Brodie's primary caregiver since she was a stay-at-home mom, so her break came in the afternoon when I would come home from work and take Brodie on a bike ride. We found a forward-facing bike seat online that attached between the seat and the handle bars and made for an excellent therapy tool. Instead of Brodie just riding *along behind me in a seat or trailer, he was right there with me where I could be pointing things out to him and engaging him the whole time. Meanwhile, Alisha was home getting some much needed time alone.*

If you are a single parent, there's no question your job will be a little tougher, so it will be even more important for you to make a deliberate effort to find ways to have time off. You may start out strong and feel like you don't need the breaks, but in the long run burnout is inescapable for the overachieving parent. It is vital to your child's success for you to be relieved of your duties fairly regularly. Developing a network of family or friends who can step in for you is crucial. We have learned through our experience that if you're willing to humble yourself and ask for help – or sometimes even just allow yourself to accept an offer – there are many truly good people out there who will jump at the chance to help you.

Keeping Your Marriage Healthy

I don't remember where, but one of the most motivational things I've read about being a father was that the greatest gift I could give my children was a healthy marriage with their mom. Pretty much every study out there has shown that children who come from a stable home with happily married parents have the odds on their side for success in almost every category, from avoiding drug abuse or criminal activity to success in their professional and personal lives.

One of the most important things we did was to find a way to spend time together, without our kids. Finding a baby-sitter who was up to the task of watching Brodie was difficult, but fortunately our main therapist was young, genuinely loved Brodie and was an exceptional babysitter for us. Having her come and watch Brodie allowed us to go out on occasional dates where we could step outside of our normal routine and enjoy a quiet dinner or movie together. After she married and moved on, we were able to find a couple of responsible students from our church youth group and a neighbor whose brother had autism who were wonderful with the boys and eager to learn about Brodie's special needs. Even going to church was difficult. We didn't feel comfortable leaving Brodie for what would amount to an hour and a half of non-engaged time with people unfamiliar with autism.

Consequently, for the first year or so Alisha stayed with Brodie in his Sunday school class while I went to the main service. When our pastor's wife learned of this, she offered to go in Alisha's place. So after shadowing Alisha for a couple weeks to learn how to meet Brodie's needs in that setting, for the next two years she went with Brodie to Sunday school so we could attend the church service together. What a blessing she was to us, enabling us to once again attend church together. It was hard for us to let go at first, particularly for Alisha since she was helping Brodie navigate through each and every situation in his life at that point. But just the chance to listen in church went a long way towards reducing our stress level and keeping us connected.

Another thing we did (and continue to do) to keep our relationship healthy was to get the kids on an early-to-bed schedule so we could have a couple hours alone each evening. Once we figured out this trick we were always able to stay current with each other's lives, frustrations, battles and victories (and also able to write this book!). By talking things through on a regular basis we avoided letting our stress levels get too high. We felt this time was not only essential for us, but also paved the way for Brodie's successes. To this day, our boys go to bed at around 7:30 p.m. so we can enjoy our evenings together (we stopped giving Brodie a nap to accomplish this early bedtime schedule). For a couple years, this often led to an early 6a.m. wake-up (when he slept through the night), but getting up early was a small price to pay for a healthy marriage and family.

Children can be deeply affected by divorce for the rest of their lives. Unfortunately, the divorce rate for families with special needs children is much higher than the already high average divorce rate for typical households. No doubt the stress of dealing with a special needs child is enough to exploit the weaknesses even in otherwise healthy marriages. It's therefore imperative that you do whatever you can to keep your marriage strong.

Staying Unified as Parents

Even among married parents, the mom and dad don't always see eye to eye on their child's autism program. This is an unfortunate reality that can be extremely difficult on the pro-active parent. It is important that neither partner judge one another, and that

*both parents educate themselves as much as possible.
Hopefully common ground can be reached, even if it
takes some help from the child's autism team, a trusted
friend, or even a counselor. Having someone serve as
a mediator in the process can help keep the child's
long-term well-being as the top priority.*

CHAPTER 5 –

START ENGAGING YOUR CHILD NOW

Your Child's Needs

*T*he process of getting your child into a treatment program for autism can be long and difficult. As a result, it is imperative that parents not waste this time and instead begin helping their child right away. There are many ways to do this, and once you have an idea of a few strategies to try you don't need special training to start implementing them.

We'd like to describe some of the basic things almost any parent can do to help even before meeting with a therapist. But first, you need to understand what some of the needs of a child with autism are:

- *a consistent environment*
- *structured daily activities and routines*
- *someone demanding eye contact from them before giving them what they want*
- *constant interaction with lots of invitations to communicate*

This list is by no means comprehensive, and will actually change over time as you come to know your child better and as your child begins to develop. You will also become increasingly attuned to his or her additional needs and can begin to adapt your strategies as you see fit.

TAKE ACTION:
Get Your Child Communicating

Now, let's get to some of the things you can do proactively both while you're waiting to be seen by an evaluator and as your child begins to receive therapy. There are many tangible ways to start helping your child in the interim before you are assigned a speech therapist, who once involved will be able to guide you through the process of helping your child step by step.

Receptive Language

Some of the first strategies we implemented in working with Brodie were drawn from a book titled, <u>Let Me Hear Your Voice</u>, by Catherine Maurice. In this book we began reading about the lack of understanding children with autism have for receptive language. Receptive language is defined as the ability to understand or comprehend language. For example, if you say to your son, "Go get your shoes," and he responds by going to get his shoes, he very likely has receptive language skills. If he doesn't respond he may be lacking in this area of communication.

To improve Brodie's receptive language skills we began implementing a few simple strategies. First, rather than modeling adult speech for Brodie, we began limiting our statements to one or possibly two word phrases (e.g. 'come,' 'all done,' 'open' or 'in'). In response to this change, we noticed Brodie beginning to understand some of these simple commands.

By breaking down phrases into smaller fragments, our goal was for Brodie to first learn to understand words, then learn to mimic parts of words, and ultimately, to use whole words spontaneously in his own speech.

Association Tools

Additionally, we also learned from the speech pathologist to associate an object with an event as often as possible. For example, every night at bath time we brought Brodie's frog bath toy and handed it to him (bath time was the only time the frog toy came out). After roughly a week of this, Brodie began to take the frog from our hand and race down the hall to the bathroom where he'd throw the frog in the tub, excited for his bath time. This was an amazing development to us, as Brodie had previously only recognized bath time when we physically took him to the tub. After this breakthrough, we began associating car keys with 'going' and Brodie's favorite blanket with 'bedtime.' Making these changes helped us communicate with Brodie more effectively and eventually gave Brodie the tools he would need to make his own requests.

PECS- Picture Exchange Communication System

As the next step toward verbal communication, our therapists helped us implement a behavioral therapy tool called PECS - Picture Exchange Communication System - both at school and at home. This system is based on picture cue cards that are used in place of words in order to express the child's desires as well as to communicate daily schedules and/or routines.

When we first started using PECS our therapists recommended that we place some of Brodie's favorite toys up out of his reach on shelves in his bedroom. The therapists took pictures of these toys and made them into small cards that we placed with Velcro on the front of the toy shelf at his level so that Brodie could use the pictures to request a toy. Each picture cue was very visible and easy for him to pull off. The goal was to train Brodie to bring the picture cue card to one of us to request a desired toy. Since the toy was sitting on a high shelf, he couldn't reach it himself and was forced to get help.

We started this process by introducing a card to Brodie when we played with that particular toy or activity. For example, as Brodie sat down to stack his towers I would show Brodie the small picture cue of that toy and say, "Look Brodie, towers," (while pointing to the picture). We also started using the picture cues to make schedules and posted cards such as the 'potty' or 'drink' cards around our home so Brodie could communicate those specific needs. This system worked so well for Brodie that we ended up expanding its use. We began using it for long car trips, church, babysitters and even running errands. We would make schedule strips using pictures of every place we went, including the local stores we frequented, friends' houses, church and anywhere else we would go. Creating schedules using PECS cards significantly reduced Brodie's anxiety in what had been extremely stressful situations for him. To this day, written schedules are highly beneficial for Brodie and we continue to use them in new or difficult situations. We've found them to be especially useful while on vacation, when the schedule is noticeably different and often changes several times a day.

While we are not suggesting that you try to teach yourself the PECS system without the assistance of a trained autism therapist, we can recommend beginning this process of using cues in your home. Even the simple task of associating a picture of a toy with the actual, physical toy can help your child make the connection between pictures and objects (e.g. a picture of a train and a toy train). This can be a very difficult concept for children with autism to comprehend.

Early-Learning Video/DVD Tools

Early-learning videos were also a big help for Brodie. We used the "Baby Einstein" and "Baby Bumblebee" video series and had very good success with both. Since we weren't giving Brodie any downtime from interaction at this early stage, these videos were a great opportunity for Brodie to have some time away from structured therapy while still being presented with a chance to learn. One of the best times of day for this was just following his afternoon therapy session while dinner was being prepared.

During this time one of us was always in the room with Brodie trying to prompt communication and keep him from 'stimming' (unusual, repetitive behavior) during the video. At this point in time, Brodie's stims included running in circles around our coffee table while flapping his hands, checking in at the corner of the room periodically (placing his back to the corner and looking around the room) and grinding his teeth. Since we had a Great Room floor plan Alisha could stay in tune with Brodie while cooking meals if no one else was around, and jump in to redirect him if he started to stim while watching the video.

Interaction Techniques

We also made a habit of pausing the video every couple minutes or so to ask Brodie questions based on his developmental level. Some of these questions included, "Brodie, what is that?", "What do you see?", and/or commands such as, "Say plane." Brodie was eager to interact with us knowing that as soon as he did he was rewarded with the video continuing. Over time, we saw how much Brodie really was learning from these videos.

Generalization Skills

From the Baby Bumblebee videos, Brodie started to acquire the skill of generalization (i.e. recognizing an object in a variety of settings and forms). For example, the video would show a pig and say the word 'pig' *and then go on to show many different forms of pigs including a puzzle piece of a pig, a drawing of a pig, a stuffed toy pig, etc. Though this skill was being taught in therapy as well, he was getting to practice it over and over again on his own as he watched these videos many times through.*

Intellectual Learning

Brodie also learned to spell from both of these video series. We found this out shortly after he had turned three. While driving in the car one day he randomly said aloud, "T-I-G-E-R spells tiger!" Stunned, Alisha began asking him to spell different animals, and sure enough he could do it. To this day he is still intrigued with spelling new words. As he got a little older, he also began watching these same videos in Spanish and French. These videos became great assets during long car trips.

TAKE ACTION: Get Your Child Socializing

Reinforcers

Avoiding both eye contact and social interaction with others were two of the earliest indicators of autism we observed in Brodie (at about three months of age). Consequently, one of the first changes we made in addressing these behaviors was to elicit Brodie's eye contact using different reinforcers (highly desired items). For Brodie, these included words of praise, singing songs, books, food treats, musical toys, hide-and-seek, and watching 'Veggie-Tales' or 'Baby Einstein' videos. We started using these reinforcers as rewards when he met certain goals, such as finishing a task or giving eye contact. For instance, if either of us began singing one of Brodie's favorite songs, and Brodie looked away, we would stop singing. When he re-initiated eye contact, we resumed singing again.

When reading books together, we applied a similar strategy. We would read a couple of pages out of a book Brodie was familiar with and then stop, waiting for him to look up at us before continuing. We played a different game with food treats or musical toys as reinforcers, using the phrase, "Brodie look!" When he made eye contact or looked at the displayed object, we responded with, "Good look," and handed him the treat or played the musical toy. Using these methods not only created fun and positive experiences for Brodie, but also led to dramatic improvements in both his eye contact and awareness of other people. The reinforcers were also a way of connecting with him, as there was an element of communication and mutual interaction in the simple act of providing him with something he wanted. As time went on, we were also able to use these reinforcers when teaching him to initiate requests because they were highly desired items.

Restructuring the Environment/Schedule

Restructuring Brodie's environment so there were people around him at all times, and reworking his schedule to include therapy in all settings, were other strategies we implemented. This decision was based on current research showing that children with autism who receive at least 25 hours a week of intense treatment make the most significant developmental gains.[7] In order to implement this new schedule, we all but *eliminated Brodie's independent play-time. Every waking hour became an opportunity for engaging him in some kind of social interaction. See Appendix C for a couple of examples of Brodie's daily schedules at different points in time.*

A great deal of our time with Brodie was spent in 'floor time' which provided him with developmentally appropriate activities and interaction with an adult. In other words, we spent time playing with him using toys and games that were appropriate for his age level and understanding. During floor time we worked on keeping Brodie focused, playing with toys appropriately (e.g. driving the truck instead of spinning the wheels), taking turns, requesting a toy using eye contact or picture cues, and finishing various tasks (e.g. putting shapes in a bucket – again, as described above, we would only use the single word 'in' to work on his receptive language skills).

Teaching Socially Acceptable Behavior

As you work with your child you will also come to recognize what a literal world he or she lives in. Kids with autism tend to do and say exactly what they think with none of the cynicism, sarcasm, or unfortunately sometimes, tact that are a common part of communication in our society. Their world is black and white, so when Brodie saw someone litter while we were in Amsterdam on our way to Uganda he remarked, "All Europeans litter!" Another time after being introduced to a woman with a short haircut, he addressed her saying, "Hello Mr. Helen!"

Of course, even typical children will exhibit this kind of bluntness, but they also have the ability to eventually learn more acceptable social behaviors naturally (oftentimes despite their parents!). We are constantly explaining different social graces to Brodie so he will better adapt to his environment. For example, we put in a considerable effort to teach him that it's not appropriate to ask everyone in the store how old they are, and that it's not necessary to tell everyone in the room what time it is on a minute by minute basis! All of these little personality quirks that you'll have to work through to help them better adapt socially make for some very entertaining and endearing moments!

TAKE ACTION:
Start Attacking Sensory Stimulants

As we did more research, we became aware that children with autism commonly suffer from **Sensory Integration Dysfunction.** *That is, they often have an impaired ability to properly process incoming information (e.g. things they see, hear, taste, smell or touch). As their brains process these various environmental stimuli, three basic senses are utilized:* **tactile, vestibular, and proprioceptive.**

Tactile Dysfunction

The body's tactile system interprets soft touch, pain, temperature and pressure. Signs of tactile dysfunction may include adverse reactions to certain textures in food or clothing, activities such as brushing teeth, or walking on grassy or sandy surfaces.

Vestibular Dysfunction

Vestibular dysfunction can cause either hypersensitive (over-reactive) or hyposensitive (under-reactive) responses to activities involving bodily motion, such as swinging or sliding. Children who are hypersensitive may appear fearful of movement or clumsy, while those who are hyposensitive may fixate on excessive sensory actions such as spinning or jumping.

Proprioceptive Dysfunction

The proprioceptive system provides the signals that allow an individual to sit in a chair or climb a staircase. According to the Center for the Study of Autism, some common signs of proprioceptive dysfunction are clumsiness, a tendency to fall, a lack of awareness of body position in space, odd body posturing, minimal crawling when young, difficulty manipulating small objects (buttons, snaps), eating in a sloppy manner, and resistance to new motor movement activities.[8]

Because children with autism can show varying degrees of symptoms in each of these areas of development, it is imperative that you become an expert on your child. By increasing or decreasing these sensory stimulants, you can begin to help your child better cope with their environment.

Desensitization

As you observe your child, take note of his or her reaction to different environmental factors, such as bright lights, crowded rooms, perfumes, and varying textures such as grass and sand - children with sensory integration problems commonly refuse to walk bare-footed on grass or sand. It is therefore important to try to desensitize them as much as possible by carefully exposing them to these sensory stimulants.

While this should be a part of their autism program once they're receiving professional help, you can get started (cautiously!) by doing some simple things:

1) *Give your child as much physical affection as he or she can stand. Don't force anything, but repeatedly request hugs or hold hands with him or her.*

2) *Take your child out to crowded places from time to time to see how he or she responds. Be sure to note any changes in eye-contact, hyperactivity or attentiveness during these outings to help you understand his or her weak areas.*

3) *Let your child listen to all types of children's and classical music in the car and around the house.*

This not only helps them get used to different sounds, but can also ready their brain for learning.

4) Expose your child to many different textures, such as sand, shaving cream, water, mud, gooey or sticky play toys. Keep in mind that after any one of these activities you may need to provide your child a calming activity to help regain his or her ability to focus (for Brodie, tickling his back usually does the trick).

With Brodie, we implemented a multitude of strategies focusing on his sensory integration issues. Oftentimes we would need to sabotage him in ways we thought would help him break through a certain intolerance or irritation to sensory input. To this day, we continue to work with him in areas of sensory integration where we suspect an issue.

For example, Brodie used to avoid touching sand at all costs. To tackle this issue, one of his therapists taught us to hide pieces from one of Brodie's favorite puzzles in the sandbox so he'd have to dig them out in order to finish it. Brodie also used to panic whenever he was squirted with water. Since we knew this would be a popular activity for his brothers one day, we began to initiate some family water fights in the backyard. Though he hated it at first, over time he got used to it and now he's one of the first to grab a water gun! While issues like this certainly can affect typical children as well, the problems are heightened with autism and may demand more of your time to help your child practice appropriate ways to react in such situations.

We should note that the area of sensory integration was the most difficult area of therapy for us to understand. Our occupational therapist was instrumental in helping us learn about Brodie's needs, and then designing a program to address them. We've also seen that sensory issues can come and go, surface in different environments, and then reappear after a period of insensitivity. But overall, if you stay on top of the issues as they arise, their sensitivity to all different kinds of stimulants certainly can be reduced and even eliminated in many instances.

TAKE ACTION: Learn How to Discipline your Child with Autism

This is undoubtedly the most difficult section of the book for us to write, as it continues to be a work in progress with Brodie. Disciplining typical children is difficult enough, let alone a child with special needs. Further complicating matters is the fact that there is no limit to the number of differing philosophies on discipline out there. We feel like we would be better equipped to write this section after our kids are grown and out of the house! But as it relates to raising a child with autism, discipline is no doubt at the top of most parents list of concerns they want advice and help with, so we will share some of the things we've learned so far along the way.

First, we would encourage parents to avoid using the words 'no' and "don't" when disciplining. By no means does this mean to give your child their way on everything. Rather, simply refrain from focusing on the negative and telling them what not to do. We have found that telling Brodie what he shouldn't do is basically programming him to repeat that action. One ther-

apist explained it to us as their brain working like a card file. So if Brodie has just squeezed the cat, his brain is stuck on the 'card' for squeezing the cat. So if we tell him, "Don't squeeze the cat" we haven't done anything to change the card he's focused on. On the other hand, if we instead redirect him and tell him, "Do gentle to the cat" (and have him practice), we have reprogrammed his brain to think about being gentle. This has probably been the most significant thing that has helped us in disciplining Brodie.

Another thing we've done is to have Brodie practice correct behavior after situations where he's made a bad choice. For example, if we tell him to go sit on a time-out and he throws a fit and screams on the way there, we will calmly bring him back to where he was and practice doing it the right way. Often, we will have to bring him back 3 or 4 times before he does it right. But the more he practices doing the behavior correctly, he begins to get into the habit of doing it that way.

Finally, positive reinforcement is far more important that punishing them for their mistakes (though punishment – usually in the form of withholding a privilege - still has to play a role in some situations, depending on how far developed your child is). We've implemented positive incentives both at home and school in a variety of ways. For example, we use a grading scheme for his school days. He either gets a green, yellow or red report from his teacher depending on how his day went in the classroom. After a pre-determined number of green days in a row, he earns some kind of prize that is highly attractive to him. The prize can change as his desires or interests change, and we allow him to change it ahead of time if he desires. Currently, he earns a motorcycle ride with me around our neighborhood here in Africa if he gets three green days in a row. We have seen an amazing improvement in his behavior at school since we implemented this system.

Obviously, this is not a comprehensive guide to disciplining a child with autism. We have yet to find a truly good resource for this, and given the complexity of the issue there is little doubt as to why such resources are scarce. In our home, we have tried to create an environment where Brodie can access choices when he's faced with a potentially troublesome situation. We remind him often of things he can choose to do if he needs time away from his brothers or even us. He has activities in his room that calm him (puzzle books and other thinking games that seem to calm him down) and we often distinguish between sending him for a break and for a time-out. His breaks are an opportunity for him to self-regulate, and then return to the family once he feels ready, whereas with a time-out we are in control of when he may return. But for parents, two critical values to embody no matter who the child is are patience and consistency. For parents of a child with autism, these two traits are even more important.

TAKE ACTION:
Ensure Your Child's Progress

Adapting Your Strategies

The baby steps we saw Brodie take early on were all the fuel we needed to forge ahead, full steam. As early as a few days after implementing the autism strategies we had learned, we started seeing improvements in his eye-contact, attentiveness and tolerance of certain sensory activities, such as squishing clay. Our families noticed too, as Brodie was beginning to look at them and acknowledge their presence or words. Though

Brodie's ability to speak was still several months away, it was clear to us that we were laying the ground-work for his future communication. As we saw him improving we also found it necessary to adapt our teaching strategies quite frequently. You will find that periodically reevaluating and adapting your strategies to meet your child's changing abilities will be crucial to his or her development.

Communicating: Narration

As you recognize your child improving in different areas it will be your job to initiate more advanced conversations and interactions in order to ensure your child's continued progress. For instance, as your child begins to understand receptive language (i.e. what others are saying to him or her), you will need to adapt accordingly the way you communicate. As Brodie improved in his ability to understand spoken language and use simple words like "in" and "push" we encouraged him with phrases like, "Brodie, look, cat!... Say 'cat'!" (while pointing at our cat). The important thing to remember is that without continual opportunities to communicate, it is highly unlikely that your child will simply 'catch' language from what is going on around him or her.

Over time your one and two-word statements (ex. "Brodie look") should evolve into a constant narration of daily events. Once you notice your child understanding more complicated phrases and one-step directions like, "Bring me the ball," you can begin to:

- *point out everything you see to your child ("Look up at the airplane!")*
- *acknowledge your actions ("We're waiting our turn at the stoplight.")*
- *tell where you're going ("Brodie, we are driving to the mall.")*
- *give reasons for your actions ("I'm changing brother's diaper because it's dirty.")*
- *narrate your child's actions ("You are putting all the blocks in...now you are pouring them all out.")*

At the same time you are constantly engaging your child in some form of communication or interaction with another person, you will also be limiting the down time in your child's schedule. Restricting your child's alone time will in turn help eliminate opportunities for stim- ming (ex. hand-flapping, head shaking) as well as help ensure that you are capitalizing on his or her learning opportunities. As your opportunities for teaching language expand it is very helpful to consult weekly with your child's speech therapist. Sharing about your child's improvements and asking for help with the next step should help you learn how to implement the most effective strategies possible for teaching your child language.

Offering Constant Praise

Many times as parents we underestimate the power of praise. However, rewarding your child with praise for their actions and speech will be well worth the extra effort. If your child loves sweets then your praise may come in the form of something as simple as a raisin given as a reinforcer for an attempt at communication. With Brodie we found that squishing him on the couch with a pillow until he giggled was a great way to both praise him and elicit eye contact. Each day when I would come home from work I would lay Brodie on the couch (he was two years old at the time) and wait until he made eye contact with me. When he did, I would squish him with a pillow, and say, "Good looking!" Each time I stopped, I waited for Brodie to make eye contact again, and then repeated the process. Sometimes this game would go on for several minutes. All the while, Brodie had no idea he was actually doing therapy with me.

Providing these types of interactions with your child even if they've never spoken a word will prepare them for future speech development. At the beginning, making a single sound is worthy of high praise for children who struggle with speech. Don't be too stingy with your praise! Phrases such as, "Brodie good job," "Awesome," "Nice work," and, "Yay for Brodie" were constants in our home and worked well to encourage Brodie in his hours of therapy. Months later, as Brodie's speech developed, we were often reminded of how important praise is as we heard Brodie begin to recognize his own nice work. Pretty soon we began to hear him say things like, "Brodie did it," and "Do it again" as he played nearby. Try to remember you're rewarding any attempt at communication no matter how slight, not evaluating their proper pronunciation or phraseology!

In the beginning, you will essentially be having a one-person conversation at all times. But the more you use these strategies of teaching communication, the more aware they'll become that you're talking to them, even if they're showing no signs of paying attention. It definitely takes some getting used to – that is, pointing out everything and explaining everything going on around you. We often remarked to each other how obnoxious we must've appeared in public explaining even the most trivial of things to Brodie (e.g. "Brodie, the lady said 'hi'. Look up. Say, 'hi.' "). We dubbed ourselves 'super-parents', making fun of what others must've thought were absurdly over-bearing tactics! It didn't matter to us though, as the world of autism is one place where 'over-parenting' is not only effective, it's necessary.

The Importance of Consistent Home Therapy

As parents, we strongly believe that the consistency and intensity we put into Brodie's home therapy early on not only improved his eye contact and attention span, but also positively influenced his attachment toward both of us. We were also very encouraged by *the "baby steps" we witnessed in Brodie's social and language development in the first several weeks, even though his home therapy services had yet to begin.*

Brodie's skills improved significantly in the couple of months between his initial evaluation and his final acceptance into the early intervention program (age birth to three years). So much so in fact that the therapist conducting the evaluation confided to us that she was glad she'd seen him early on. As she explained it, younger children are already difficult to diagnose for autism, so coupled with the fact that some of his indicators for autism had been watered down by our home therapy, she would've had a difficult time diagnosing him for services. We were very encouraged that our hard work was already paying dividends, even before a substantial therapy regimen had begun.

Balancing Professional and Home Therapy

While any parent knows their child better than their doctor or teacher, having a special needs child requires an even greater understanding of your child's needs and abilities. With autism, this is never more the case, particularly because there is such potential for improvement. Even if your child ends up receiving the recommended 25 to 30 hours a week of therapy, you will always play a crucial role in managing the therapy your child needs. If you are in tune with every aspect of your child's development, from communication deficits to sensory needs, the therapy implemented will be far more beneficial and the potential for success higher as you work with the team to target your child's weak areas.

If, on the other hand, your child receives less than the recommended hours a week of therapy, your ability and know-how to provide the additional therapy needed become essential in making up for those lost hours. For our family, therapy simply became a way of life and a new way of parenting. As we mentioned earlier, though our over-parenting habits were surely observed by those around us, from Brodie's standpoint, our constant narration of his actions, modeling of correct responses, and other strategies for constant engagement meant a possible avenue to understanding the world.

We think it's important to note that the therapy we implemented from early on was made possible by the fact that Alisha was able to be a stay-at-home mom.

Her being with Brodie each waking moment was a huge blessing and an invaluable asset in Brodie's success story. While we know that many will not be as fortunate as we were in having one parent at home, we would urge every family to fully exhaust all options that could possibly make this happen. Alisha essentially received training as an additional therapist for Brodie by being able to attend and observe all of his therapy sessions for those first couple of years. But regardless of your situation, the most effective way to become a true expert on your child is to learn to observe them through the eyes of an autism consultant. To accomplish this, it is important to maintain a good working relationship with your child's therapists.

We can't say it enough how blessed we were to have the therapists we had helping us. They were totally committed to Brodie's success, and proved it time and again by working with us on every little detail of Brodie's progress. They were never challenged by our desire to be a part of the therapy and strategizing, and were eager to listen to any ideas or observations we brought to the table. Many times they would stay longer than scheduled or do extra prep-work on their own time. They brought him little gifts and games, and even cool therapy toys that they picked up at the store over the weekend. All of the extra effort and love they gave showed us the special interest they had in Brodie. We will never be able to repay them for all they did to help him. Their hard work played a critical role in Brodie's success.

Referencing & Tracking

As mentioned in Chapter 3, we started a journal tracking Brodie's behavior patterns. We used the journal writings as a point of reference. By keeping a written record of Brodie's progress, Alisha was at times able to recognize instances where he might have mastered a skill during therapy time, but hadn't yet met that goal in his daily home life. On one such occasion, the therapist's data showed Brodie consistently following two-step directions such as, "Go potty and wash your hands," in the classroom setting. However, the data we were recording showed that Brodie's ability to follow through with these same types of commands at home was still sporadic. This information was valuable for his therapists to see so they would know Brodie still needed more work in this area. Time and again, our home journal was instrumental in both identifying lingering deficits and confirming that other goals had been mastered.

TAKE ACTION:
Educating Yourself and Your Child

Past Research

If you find yourself frantically researching autism because your child has been diagnosed with the disorder, consider yourself extremely blessed to be living in this day and time.

It wasn't too long ago (the 1950's and in some cases, sadly, even as late as the 1980's) that children with autism were thought by some 'experts' to be the result of cold and unloving parents, especially the mother (often referred to as the 'refrigerator mother theory'). As if being told that wasn't bad enough, some specialists would then recommend the child be sent off to live their lives in an institution because there was no hope for improvement. Even to this day, unfortunately, a few of these individuals who propagate the 'refrigerator mother theory' still exist. However, the vast majority of professionals in the field of autism today see this theory for what it is – total hogwash!

We did run across one of these 'experts' shortly after we found out about Brodie. Alisha took a special education class for her Master's degree where a guest-speaker came to speak about the connection of childhood disorders such as ADHD and autism with a poor birthing experience. The theory this speaker advocated was that a lack of connection made during the birthing process between some newborn infants and their mothers directly leads to certain behavioral disorders.

To Alisha, this sounded awfully similar to the 'refrigerator mother theory'. So she raised her hand and calmly (with smoke coming out her ears!) confronted the speaker about her claims as they related to current autism research. Not too surprisingly, the woman was not prepared for battle and even seemed comfortable with removing autism from the list of disorders impacted by her theory!

Research Today

Thankfully, those days are for the most part long gone, and these theories have been replaced by a growing number of physicians and psychologists who realize just how much potential these kids actually have when the right methods are employed by therapists and mimicked in the home by parents and caregivers. Most experts agree that at least 25 hours a week of instruction is necessary for effectively intervening into the life of a child with autism.[9] However, as parents become able to mimic the strategies used during therapy, the child will spend even less time 'off-duty'. With Brodie, we soon realized that it was in his best interest if we very rarely gave him time where he was alone without one of us initiating communication.

The modern day autism treatment plan is a complex combination of several techniques and strategies that are applied in different situations and contexts based on the individual's strengths and deficits. As a parent, it will become important that you learn these strategies from your therapists so you can provide consistency in your child's home environment. While it may seem intimidating at the start – and it certainly is a lot to know, *once you see how intuitive many of the strategies are, and especially how successful they can be, you'll have no problem finding the motivation to learn.*

Your therapists will surely aim to keep you up to speed with what they're doing as they are well aware of how important it is that you learn the core skills of the therapy they're implementing. Our therapists were always very eager to help us reinforce what they were doing with Brodie during his therapy sessions in the home, and spent countless additional hours with us modeling their techniques.

Best Practices for Teaching Children with Autism

In 2001, the National Research Council (NRC) researched and put together a list of the <u>Best Practices in Educating Children with Autism</u>.[10] These findings provide a consolidated, official catalogue of the most effective methods of teaching children with autism. Consequently, many educational programs now use this list as a basis for training their therapists. Most of these practices have many aspects to them and are always adapted to the individual. It is therefore imperative that you discuss the different strategies with your therapists to decide which ones to implement and learn the best way to do so for your child.

Applied Behavior Analysis (ABA)

One of the most widely used types of therapy is that of Applied Behavioral Analysis (ABA). Wikipedia, the online encyclopedia, defines ABA as "the systematic process of studying and modifying observable behavior through a manipulation of the environment." In short, it is a way of altering behaviors in individuals using a variety of repetitive methods. It is imperative that the person applying these methods has substantial knowledge of the characteristics of autism.

For the past several years, we relied heavily on ABA as the foundation for Brodie's therapy. Generally, ABA consists of three essential strategies that are effective in teaching receptive and expressive language: **Discrete Trial Training (DTT), Pivotal Response Training (PRT) and Functional Routines (FR).**

Discrete Trial Training (DTT)

Discrete Trial Training is excellent for teaching eceptive language. For instance, a child might be asked, "give me pig", which would require him to identify and hand the toy pig to the therapist. In this example, the pig would be the only item on the table. After this task is mastered another object would be added to the table, requiring the child to scan and discriminate between two objects and select the appropriate object. In each case, the same process is repeated several times over until each new skill is mastered. The difficulty level of the task becomes more and more challenging as the child's abilities improve.

Pivotal Response Training (PRT)

Pivotal Response Training is an effective way to teach expressive language to children with autism. This method requires the child to give a response that communicates in some way that they desire the object held by the therapist. For this method to be successful, it's important to use items that are highly desirable to the child. In the beginning, the child is simply taught to make eye contact. This skill then develops into reaching for an object, then babbling, then imitating, and finally requesting the object by name. Once you *learn the basics of what to expect of your child, this can easily be done in the home with some guidance from your child's therapist.*

Functional Routines (FR)

The receptive and expressive language skills learned in DTT and PRT are organized into activities called Functional Routines. Examples of FR's may include: washing hands, going to and from school, taking turns, mealtime, and transitioning from one activity to another. These procedures are taught multiple times and then implemented in different settings to help the child be successful throughout his or her day. They can essentially be used to teach any skill the child is struggling with.

It is important that you receive training from your therapists before trying these strategies out because subtle alterations to the techniques can negate the progress your therapists might be making. You shouldn't be intimidated by these methods since many parents have successfully learned and implemented them. However, you should strive to become as knowledgeable as possible about them so you can maximize your child's success.

CHAPTER 6 –

STEP 5:
CONSIDER DIETARY
INTERVENTION

The Basis for Dietary Intervention:

Food Intolerances

*W*e began exploring the connection between autism and the stomach when Brodie was about two years old. It wasn't that we were struggling for success. In fact, Brodie was doing exceptionally well. At that point, Brodie was receiving 18 hours a week of therapy from his program (along with the 12-15 hours Alisha was giving him) and showing steady improvement in virtually all aspects of his program.

He was nearing age-level in his gross-motor (running, climbing, etc.), fine-motor (drawing, feeding himself with utensils, pinching and grasping small objects) and cognitive skills (puzzles, problem solving), while still making up ground in the areas of expressive language (spoken words) and social skills. By all accounts his progress was outstanding. However, we were still very concerned about his chronic diarrhea and abnormal sleeping patterns, as well as the sporadic behavior problems that usually accompanied them.

Symptoms of Food Intolerance

The trends we were seeing in Brodie's stool and behavior during his first couple years of life were leading us to believe he may be having trouble with some of the foods he was eating. He also displayed a number of indicators commonly associated with food intolerance. Below is a list of some of the most common indicators of food intolerance:

- eczema
- chronic constipation or diarrhea
- seizures
- migraines

- *nightmares*
- *facial rash (red blotchy cheeks)*
- *over or under-eating habits*
- *extremely picky eating (e.g. only eats certain, particular foods)*
- *strong cravings for certain foods*
- *frequent tantrum or screaming episodes*
- *wheezing*
- *reflux*
- *abnormal sleep/waking patterns*

For more information about food intolerance, you can reference Karyn Seroussi's book titled <u>Unraveling the Mystery of Autism and Pervasive Developmental Disorder: A Mother's Story of Research & Recovery</u>.[11]

Research:

Dietary Allergens - Wheat & Dairy Products

As a result of the symptoms we saw in Brodie, we began to research the connection between diet and autism. In a series of studies from the late 1960's and early 1970's, medical professionals hypothesized that wheat and dairy products might worsen the severity of symptoms in certain behavioral disorders.[12]

In 1981, Dr. Karl Reichelt, the Director of Clinical Chemistry for the Department of Pediatric Research at the National Hospital in Oslo, Norway, found evidence clarifying the biochemical link between diet and behavioral disorders. While examining patients with autism, Dr. Reichelt discovered a pattern of abnormal peptides in their urine.[13] *These peptides, or partially broken down proteins, were 4-6 amino acids long (instead of a normal single amino acid strand) and matched the sequence of opioid peptides (as in 'opium', the drug!). The sources for these peptides were identified as gluten and casein.*

Further Research: The Intestinal Tract

Since the late 1990's, gastrointestinal specialists have also found that a vast number of children with autism have abnormally permeable intestinal membranes, enabling the opiate peptides from dietary sources to travel to the central nervous system, (CNS) thereby disturbing neurotransmission to the brain. This opioid activity in the brain can result in delayed or abnormal communicative, cognitive, and social abilities. Professionals and parents worldwide have since reported that implementing a GFCF diet can significantly decrease or even eliminate many autistic behaviors.

The work of Arthur Krigsman, MD, a pediatric gastroenterologist at the New York University School of Medicine, focused on the gastrointestinal symptoms now being associated with autism. We had the privilege of hearing Dr. Krigsman speak at the 'Defeat Autism Now!' (DAN!) Conference in Portland, Oregon, in October, 2003, where he explained the pattern of gastrointestinal problems he's found in children with autism. Reflecting on his initial findings, Dr. Krigsman stated that after examining 43 patients with autism, he found 90% of them demonstrated ileocolonic lymphoid nodular hyperplasia (LNH), a unique form of enterocolitis or inflammatory bowel disease. At the time of the conference, he had seen over 150 patients with autism and reported that the rate of occurrence of these symptoms essentially hadn't changed.[14]

Comparing the symptoms of gastrointestinal problems that Dr. Krigsman spoke of to those we had observed in Brodie convinced us that he most certainly *had gastrointestinal issues. Brodie's chronic bouts with diarrhea and malodorous stools were among the many common indicators Dr. Krigsman described. During his presentation, he also outlined the range of interventions available to children suffering from these types of problems, which varied depending on the type and location of the inflammation.*

The Gluten-free, Casein-free (GFCF) Diet

It is impossible to come up with a generic formula for every child's dietary and biomedical needs as each child will have his own sensitivities and intolerances. Common ground can be found on some of the basic essentials, however. Removing gluten (any derivative of wheat) and casein (any derivative of cow's milk) is usually the starting point for individuals with autism in need of a special diet. The **'Gluten-free, Casein-free (GFCF) Diet'** *is growing in popularity, with an increasing number of cookbooks and other resources. These developments have made us very thankful for the recent advancements in nutrition-based intervention.*

Our own research on the Gluten-free, Casein-free (GFCF) Diet led us to a variety of testimonials written by both parents and doctors touting the success of this diet in reducing symptomatic behaviors in children with autism. We reviewed a number of journal articles outlining small-scale, "single-blind" studies with promising results relating to the effects of dietary intervention in autism. A "single-blind" study is where only the doctor knows whether a patient is undergoing the new treatment being tested. This is done to help prevent bias within the study.

By contrast, a "double-blind" study is where neither the doctor nor the patient knows if the patient is receiving the treatment. Generally, "double-blind" studies are given more credence, but are also much more difficult to perform. With autism, double-blind studies are particularly difficult to conduct as parents are justifiably unwilling to spend critical weeks, months or years participating in a study where their child may not be receiving any treatment if he or she is in the control group. Because autism is a spectrum disorder with widely varying symptoms and severity, it's also nearly impossible to form a group of individuals with the same strengths and weaknesses, deficiencies and unusual behaviors.

The more we looked into the research available on children with autism and the evidence of gastrointestinal issues amongst these kids, the more convinced we were that Brodie needed help with his stomach. It was at that point that we decided the GFCF diet was the right place to start in order to help Brodie tackle his health issues.

As we looked into other common food sensitivities we discovered that corn and soy, the most popular replacements for gluten and casein, are also widely recognized in the autism community as trouble-causers, and many times are the next to go. Foods such as nuts, rice, and sugar, can stay for some children, but may also cause significant skin irritations, behavioral issues, and/or sleep disturbances for others. While our findings made Brodie's future world of food choices seem rather bleak, we were determined to get to the root of Brodie's stomach problems.

Autism & Sleep Patterns

While we've found only sparse data regarding the effects of diet on abnormal sleep patterns, many anecdotal stories indicate a possible connection in this *area as well. One such example we found in Karyn Seroussi's book, <u>Unraveling the Mystery of Autism and Pervasive Developmental Disorder</u>, in which Seroussi shares how removing casein from her daughter's diet abruptly stopped her nighttime crying, waking patterns, and complaints of her "room shaking" (her daughter did not have autism).*

Seroussi also noted that when she accidentally challenged her daughter Laura's diet with milk about eight weeks later, she woke up four times in one night after two months of sleeping through till morning with no problems. Furthermore, over the course of the following year, Seroussi reports that Laura was mistakenly given dairy four times, and that each of these episodes was followed by a wakeful night of sleep.

While Laura was a typically-developing child otherwise, her habit of frequently waking in the night reminded us of Brodie, who'd had trouble sleeping through the night since birth. He typically woke several times a night, and often started his day at 2 or 3 o'clock in the morning after being unable to go back to sleep. At the time we started him on the diet – he was two years, five months - it was a rare occasion for him to sleep soundly through the night.

Non-Dietary Allergens

We should mention here that non-dietary allergens can also affect the behavior and physical well-being of a child with autism. Products such as shaving cream, glue, markers, paint, pesticides, fertilizers, and even play dough may have ingredients that interact with your child's skin and cause behavioral symptoms to appear or intensify. Other household items such as liquid soaps, cleaners, and laundry detergent may also pose a problem for your child. More information on this topic can be found on the website www.generationrescue. org/biomedical.html. We also share more about how we approached this topic of non-dietary allergens in Chapter 7.

Treatment Options

Noting that surgery is the most extreme treatment outlined for children after all other options are exhausted, the study from Dr. Krigsman outlined previously emphasized that "a frequently overlooked but *very valuable form of therapy is dietary intervention."[15] The testimonials of parents who shared their children's dietary success stories at the DAN! conference we attended reinforced our decision to start the GFCF diet to treat Brodie's gastrointestinal problems.*

CHAPTER 7 –

STEP 7:
IMPLEMENTING
A SPECIAL DIET

Note: The dietary interventions discussed here are based on our personal experiences. We are not nutritionists nor have we been trained in the nutritional sciences. Any alteration to your child's diet should only be made after consulting with your child's physician/DAN! doctor to be certain it is appropriate for your child.

*C*reating an outline for dietary intervention is a difficult undertaking. For this reason, this chapter will be less prescriptive and more descriptive *of the approach we took and a chronicle of some of the different things we tried. By gaining insight into the thought processes leading to the decisions we made, we hope you'll be better equipped to tackle this aspect of your child's recovery process.*

After hearing numerous testimonials of families whose children showed dramatic improvements with the Gluten-free Casein-free (GFCF) diet, we were motivated to try it despite the imposition it would place on our family. So about two weeks before attending the Portland DAN! (Defeat Autism Now!) Conference in early October, 2003, we finally started Brodie on the GFCF diet at age two years and five months. Since he had struggled with chronic diarrhea and very poor sleeping habits from a very young age, we felt that his symptoms warranted this decision. This meant removing all wheat and dairy products from his diet, including all products containing even trace amounts of either. It was a monumental task.

Dairy Products: Sources of Casein

From the beginning, the prospect of removing dairy products from Brodie's diet was far easier than removing gluten since Brad has had a milk-intolerance since birth and was already aware of most products containing dairy ingredients. While some of these products are obvious (e.g. cheese, buttermilk, most margarines, cream, and cottage cheese, etc.); others are not so obvious (e.g. whey, caseinates, lactose, etc.).

Gluten

Removing gluten from Brodie's diet was a whole different story. Gluten is not only found as a common ingredient in many foods, but is also embedded within a number of other ingredients, such as kamut, rye, barley, couscous, and semolina and consequently, may not be listed clearly on some ingredients lists. To this day, we are amazed at the wide range of foods we find containing traces of gluten. Although reading the label on each product you purchase is a good start, it by no means guarantees that the item is free of a particular substance (such as gluten), unless it is explicitly written as such on the packaging.

When you're aiming to eliminate 100% of a substance, the only way to know with total certainty that it is not in a particular item is to call the manufac-

turer. Even still, it is a good idea to check back periodically with the manufacturer as processing locations or protocols can change, sometimes affecting the content of the product.

A good way to avoid buying products containing gluten and casein is to buy from organic or nutritional food brands, as these companies tend to be much more deliberate in their food production and processing since their consumers are typically more interested in such things. Another resource for GFCF foods is a book we highly recommend to anyone attempting this diet. It's called the <u>GFCF Diet Shopping Guide</u> by Judy DeHart. For the first several months on the diet, Alisha always took this guide with her to the grocery store.

Cross-Contamination

Cross-contamination (when a certain product comes in contact with an eliminated substance during processing) can be one of the trickiest parts of trying to remove a particular ingredient. One of the more random examples of cross-contamination we heard about occurred in a particular brand of raisins. When purchased in small, individual boxes, the raisins are gluten free. However, if you purchase a large bag of the same brand of raisins, the conveyor belt carrying these raisins to the bagging area during processing is dusted with flour to prevent sticking, thus contaminating the raisins with gluten! Instances such as this of cross-contamination can be extremely frustrating, especially since the reaction to even trace amounts of gluten is oftentimes every bit as extreme as that of a major violation.

Giving the Diet Time to Work

Given the difficulty of removing gluten and casein completely, we are not surprised when we hear families say that the diet didn't work for their child. After hearing more about their experience in detail, however, one of two things has usually occurred: 1) Gluten and casein were not fully removed from the child's diet, either through cross-contamination or embedded secondary ingredients; or 2) They tried the diet for only a month or two, and therefore did not allow enough time for the gluten and casein to fully work its way out of their child's system. Our DAN! doctor told us it can take several months to completely flush out gluten.

Eliminating Problem Foods

From the beginning, we've approached the diet with a consistent strategy: recognize an apparent reaction to a particular food, remove that food, make observations and add the food back in or decide to keep it out; wait for a period of relative stability (at least a week or so of good sleeping habits/behavior and well-formed stools), then challenge a new food, observe any possible negative reactions, wait two or three days and challenge the new food again and finally, make changes based on what Brodie's stomach dictates.

After more than three years on this journey, we have removed many of the foods Brodie ate when he started the GFCF diet. In addition to gluten and casein, some of the foods we've had to eliminate are products containing: preservatives, artificial colorings, soy, most cooking oils, seeds, sugar, most nuts, yeast and corn.

We cut out these foods because of the reactions we saw in Brodie, including chronic diarrhea, behavioral problems, constant hyperactivity, and poor sleeping patterns. Each time we stopped feeding Brodie a problem food we saw marked improvement in these areas within a week.

Phenolic Foods

Another change we made in Brodie's diet was based on a connection we noticed between his mood swings and eating foods that are high in phenols. We discovered this connection during one particularly hard week for Brodie. Both Tuesday and Thursday morning of that week Brodie woke up ready for the day at four o'clock. On both occasions he appeared very hyper, moody, slightly aggressive and very stimmy. He was also insistent on eating a banana!

Later that week Alisha stumbled upon several websites stating how some people with autism suffer when eating foods that are high in phenols (unique properties that can be high or low in different foods). One website, TACA (Talk About Curing Autism) stated: "High levels of phenols in certain foods seem to affect children with autism and individuals with sensitive digestive and/or immune systems."[16] Different foods have different levels of phenols. Foods like bananas, red grapes, apples, tomatoes, and many food dyes have a higher phenolic content. As the body struggles to process these phenolic compounds it can cause a multitude of symptoms including night-waking, irrita-

bility, night sweats, eczema, aggressive behavior and dark circles under the eyes.

The behaviors we witnessed in Brodie were consistent with these findings. The next morning we started avoiding these highly phenolic foods in Brodie's diet. In just two days, he was noticeably calmer. Alisha's parents came to visit the following weekend and reported that he was the calmest they'd seen him. We continue to monitor Brodie's behavior in relation to his phenol intake and make adjustments accordingly, though we have not completely removed these foods from his diet as he seems to tolerate them in moderate quantities.

More Red Flags: Non-Dietary Allergens

After a couple of months of having Brodie on the GFCF diet, we began to question whether or not other products in our house were also problematic for Brodie. Early on, our thought was that as long as Brodie wasn't actually eating anything he reacted to he would be fine. We were wrong!

By default we discovered that even the allergens that come into contact with his skin make their way to *his bloodstream. One day, after picking up Brodie from pre-school we noticed he was acting very odd. He was jumpy, avoiding eye contact, and making a lot of loud noises. While we could not think of any change or violation in his diet, we knew something had definitely gone wrong. The therapists confirmed that Brodie had not eaten anything other than the snack Alisha had sent with him to school.*

As Alisha talked with Brodie's therapists the following day, one of them mentioned that Brodie had played with cornmeal in the classroom the previous morning. From that point on, we watched very closely what Brodie touched both at home and at school, and confirmed that his body was definitely reacting to products that came into contact with his skin (e.g. shaving cream, glue, paint, corn meal, play-dough, etc.) For this reason, we began investigating other household products such as liquid soaps, cleaners, baby wipes and laundry detergent as well.

Unfortunately, our research on home products showed that many of the common household items we were using for Brodie were not GFCF. We discovered that even things as simple as a sticker or stamp could contain gluten and pose a problem if placed in contact with Brodie's skin. While it's hard to know to what degree each of these items effects Brodie's system, our experience taught us that contact with even trace amounts of gluten or casein can be problematic.

Food Replacements

By far the most important resource we had in starting the GFCF diet was a local autism consultant in town who offered to meet Alisha at the grocery store. The consultant had Alisha bring a list of each food Brodie ate, and then walked her down the aisles in the nutrition section of the store. Alisha was able to find GFCF replacements for most all the foods on her list, such as different types of flour to substitute with when baking, deli meats, and several alternative snack foods. It was definitely the jump-start we needed to tackle this intimidating endeavor.

Once we had some ingredients picked out, the book titled Special Diets for Special Kids by Lisa Lewis offered many recipes for a variety of foods such as homemade cookies, blueberry muffins, and rice crispy treats. Later, as we began to remove more and more foods from Brodie's diet, we were forced to come up with many of our own recipes to cater to Brodie's specific needs (a list of some of these recipes can be found at the back of this book in Appendix A).

After we were confident we had removed all traces of gluten and casein (though we later learned we hadn't quite reached 100% GFCF due to household stuff like lotions, shampoo, etc.), we began looking at other foods that could be causing Brodie problems. We did this with the assistance of our DAN! doctor, Dr. John Green, at the Evergreen Center near Portland, Oregon. Dr. Green's office administered a food panel on Brodie along with several blood tests. Based on the results of these tests, we decided to further eliminate peanut butter, apples and nuts from Brodie's already GFCF diet.

Over the next year and a half, further testing along with our perception of Brodie's reactions to certain foods led us to remove corn, rice, potatoes, sugar and beans. At that point Brodie was essentially eating: pure meats, fruits, vegetables, small amounts of honey, tapioca and garbanzo/fava bean flours. We felt this restrictive diet was the only way to cleanse Brodie's system of all the foods causing him so many problems. We did clear this decision with Brodie's DAN! doctor to ensure we weren't doing something potentially harmful to Brodie. At his direction, we also increased Brodie's supplements to include the vitamins or minerals lacking in his diet.

As we worked in conjunction with Dr. Green on healing Brodie's intestinal tract with various supplements, infusions, and further testing, we finally reached a point where it was appropriate to start adding back in some of these eliminated foods. What a milestone and answer to prayer!

While we realize that gluten and casein are most likely gone for life based on what Dr. Green has taught us, our goal is to reintroduce as many foods as possible as Brodie becomes better able to digest them. This is a slow process that happens only as Brodie gets older and his intestinal tract heals. So far, over the course of the last five years on the diet, we have successfully added in foods including: tapioca flour, garbanzo flour, some beans, macadamia nuts, hazelnuts, rice, date sugar, potatoes, and coconut milk.

At Dr. Green's suggestion, when we try adding a previously eliminated food we do so in moderate amounts, offering the food once every two or three days. We also try to give Brodie the food in its most natural state. The goal is for the new food to succeed, so overloading his system with large amounts, or processed forms of the reintroduced food could reverse the progress he's made. If Brodie's behavior, stool, or sleep patterns change for the worst in conjunction with the new food, we usually eliminate it promptly. If however, we do not see any change in these areas, we may continue to offer that food as part of Brodie's diet.

Encouraging Your Child to Eat

During the first few months on the diet we had some trouble getting Brodie to eat what we put in front of him. This process took time and determination. For instance, when we first started the GFCF diet, we couldn't get him to eat peas. As a two year-old Brodie loved canned corn or green beans, but would not eat fresh peas. Unfortunately, when our DAN! doctor told us to avoid canned foods due to the extremely high *level of tin in his system, we had to remove these foods as we weren't sure where the tin was coming from.*

We decided to introduce peas by placing them on Brodie's dinner plate one night without saying anything. That first night, he wouldn't even look at them. After a few days of repeating this process we told Brodie to take the peas off his plate and put them back in the serving bowl if he wasn't going to eat them.

Finally, on day fifteen, Brodie looked at his plate and said, "French peas!" (referring to a Veggie Tales Video) and then proceeded to eat every last pea on his plate! From that day on, he has loved peas and often eats them frozen as a special treat.

We went through this same process when introducing fresh green beans. Each time we presented a new food, it seemed to take fewer times before Brodie would eat it. Months later we noticed Brodie's changing attitude toward new foods. To this day, he gets very excited to try new foods, whether it's a new vegetable, fruit, different kind of meat, or pretty much anything we put in front of him.

In settings outside our home, Brodie also grew to do exceptionally well with his diet. For instance, while snack-time at school was initially a concern for us, we've seen that even this does not faze Brodie. He may ask, "I'm not allowed to eat those kind of nuts, right?", or "Is that 'gluten-bread'?" when he sees a new food. If he's told that it wouldn't be good for his stomach, he'll carry on eating his own snack without much further thought.

On occasions when there is a birthday cake or ice cream at school, Alisha will send Brodie's type of cake or special homemade "ice cream" made with fruit and coconut milk for him to eat during the party. Brodie loves this of course. In fact, oftentimes even the other students are more interested in eating Brodie's ice cream than the treat provided. This is all to say that the battle can be won, but the earlier you start the easier it will be for your child to adapt to his or her new way of eating.

Challenging or Introducing New Foods

When challenging new foods, there are a couple of ground rules we stick to. The first thing we make sure of is that we're starting from a clean slate. For Brodie, this means his stool and sleeping/behavior patterns have been stable for at least a week, or hopefully two.

Once he reaches this point, we try adding in the new food in a modest portion.

Deciding When to Test New Foods

Adding the new food during the morning hours has always worked best for us since it gives us the entire day to observe Brodie's behavior. As Brodie has gotten older, we will often use Saturday morning for this purpose, since Brodie is at home, rather than at school. If his stomach is unable to tolerate the new food, Brodie usually becomes what we call 'loopy' within an hour.

For Brodie, 'Loopy' means he's unable to focus, extremely hyperactive, and essentially acts (and even makes faces) like he's a different kid. We've often commented that he appears to be hallucinating during these times. Diarrhea, sleep disturbances, and some-times a rash on his face or buttocks invariably accompany these behavioral problems as well – usually appearing within twenty-four hours. The symptoms he displays in reaction to a "bad food" can last anywhere from one day to up to a week, or even more.

On occasion, there have been times when it's taken up to three days for Brodie to react to a challenged food. When we added in cashew nuts, for instance, we gave Brodie a handful of plain, unsalted cashews on a Saturday and then not again until Tuesday. While he seemed to be doing great for the first couple of days, by Tuesday evening, after the second handful of nuts, he was getting pretty hyper. The hyperactivity was then followed by the sleep and stool problems described previously. As a result, we gave up on cashews for the time being. Adding in new foods while taking others out remains an ongoing process in our household.

Making Mistakes

There are also the rare instances when we have unwittingly added in a problematic food for Brodie. On one occasion, Alisha bought a bag of frozen berries at a different store than we usually shop at because we had run out during the week. After eating some at breakfast, Brodie went to school. By the time school was out two hours later, he was in his own world, unable to stop fidgeting. The therapists reported that he had a pretty rough time at school that day, and his behavior got progressively worse as the afternoon wore on. A couple of days later, we discovered the culprit. The list *of ingredients on the frozen berries also listed 'liquid sugar.' The experience was a not-so-subtle reminder of why we stay completely away from processed sugar in Brodie's diet.*

The Up & Down Cycle of Removing Problem Foods

When we first began the process of removing problem foods, the periods of improvement would last for a short time - anywhere from a few days to a few weeks - during which time Brodie seemed generally calmer, had a longer attention span, slept better, and seemed more agreeable. Our DAN! doctor explained to us that unfortunately one problem food can mask other ones, so that when one is removed, the period of improvement is short-lived due to another problem-food emerging.

When these short-term periods of progress passed, the diarrhea returned and Brodie became easily agitated, unable to focus, hyperactive, and woke frequently in the night. In addition, we noted Brodie's increased level of stimulatory behaviors (e.g. spinning, shaking his head) and a need for increased sensory input (e.g. being thrown up in the air or squashed with pillows).

The continued peaks and valleys in Brodie's development led us to conclude that there were still more hidden allergens causing these abnormal behaviors and symptoms. Yet, as this roller-coaster ride of behavior patterns repeated over and over, we were also encouraged by the fact that the spurts of improvement seemed to be more frequent and longer-lasting.

Siblings on the GFCF Diet

The way Brodie eats has greatly affected the rest of our family, particularly his two younger brothers. About a year into the process, we decided to start Jonah (our second son) on the diet as well. We did this for a couple of reasons. Most importantly, we were seeing gastrointestinal symptoms that included reflux and sporadic diarrhea that led us to believe Jonah might be suffering from some of the same food sensitivities, even though he was developing typically otherwise. At this point he was just a few months old, and his doctor had also run several tests searching for the cause of his persistent wheezing.

The other reason for starting Jonah on Brodie's diet had to do with avoiding the complications of having our boys eating different foods. Preparation time and effort was certainly a concern, but more importantly we wanted to avoid situations where Brodie would have to watch his younger brothers eat foods that he couldn't have.

As time passed, we eventually have added gluten and casein back into the younger boys' diets since the symptoms of food sensitivities they were showing subsided with age. However, even now (Brodie age seven), when we offer something 'different' to the younger boys we make sure to serve Brodie a comparable food to eat with them. For example, when the other two have French toast, Brodie gets to have it too except with homemade gluten-free bread and honey for syrup.

Our youngest son, Graysen, who was also typically developing, had trouble with milk as an infant and younger toddler. But as was the case with Jonah, we were able to add dairy products back in (at age 3 for Graysen, and age 4 1/2 for Jonah). To be sure that his body was getting the right nutrition while he was off milk, we supplemented with calcium powder and vita-mins. To this day, we supplement all three boys' diets with vitamins, calcium powder and fish oil.

Eating Out on the GFCF Diet

One of the more challenging parts to the diet is finding a way to eat out, depending on which foods you have eliminated. Fast food is not really an option, and many restaurants are unable to assure their patrons that no cross-contamination will occur in the prepara-tion process.

If gluten and casein are the only things being avoided, then finding restaurants is not as challenging. Avoiding casein is definitely doable on your own by simply avoiding dairy products on the menu. In recent years, many restaurants have also started offering gluten-free menus to assist customers with gluten intol-erances, such as those suffering from Celiac's Disease. However - and this is part of our challenge with Brodie's diet - as you remove more and more foods the prospect of eating out becomes more and more difficult.

We have found one chain restaurant in town – 'Red Robin' – where we can still go out to eat from time to *time. Our boys love the atmosphere of eating there so we were excited when our local 'Red Robin' recently began offering gluten-free hamburger patties and fries. When we eat there Brodie orders a beef patty wrapped in lettuce with mustard, endless fries without seasoning salt, and a side of cantaloupe. He loves it! However, it's important to note that just because one restaurant in a chain offers certain foods as gluten-free does not mean all the restaurants in that chain follow that same protocol!*

For example, we have been to other 'Red Robin' restaurants where the fries are not gluten-free. In this case the problem is with the fryer, where the battered (i.e. gluten) chicken or fish is fried in the same fryer as the French fries. Again, as is the case with supermarket food, the only way to know for sure is to call ahead and speak with the manager. For special assistance, you can also call the national office of the restaurant chain to help direct you to acceptable menu items. A follow-up call to the local branch (of the chain restaurant) is also very wise since variations in protocols are common.

When traveling overnight, most hotels can provide you with a microwave and refrigerator even if your room does not have one. We have also used a portable, electric burner to cook or warm foods right in our room. At one hotel a friend of ours was even allowed to use the kitchen to cook her son's meals.

Having the Right Perspective

Many families have had an even harder time than we had with Brodie when it came to changing his diet. We've heard stories of kids who have self-limited their diets in bizarre ways. Several kids we've heard about will only eat orange-colored foods (this is actually a common occurrence within the autism community). Others outright refuse to eat foods with certain textures, even to the point of gagging themselves. For each child with food sensitivities it may be something different.

But in any case, this can be a very frustrating process for the one trying to feed them. There were times in the beginning when Alisha was pushed to the point of tears over Brodie refusing to eat certain foods. Coupled with our guilt over the fact that he was 'missing out' on many of the common treats kids enjoy, these were some very tough times.

Going through this process, we found comfort in something Karyn Seroussi said at the DAN! Conference we attended in Portland. She said that by giving gluten and casein to a kid with a 'leaky gut' (a term commonly used when describing the poor absorption in the stomachs of individuals with autism), "you might as well be pouring paint down his throat!" We remind ourselves of this whenever we start feeling badly for keeping Brodie on his special diet.

We also remember how well he eats and how his diet is far and away the healthiest of any kid's that we've seen. We were reminded of this at a friend's party one Halloween. When the piñata was broken, our boys emerged from the pile of candy bars with huge smiles, each clutching boxes of raisins in both fists!

Importance of Consistency

Even on holidays or other tempting occasions, we never intentionally violate the diet unless we are reintroducing a food. There are no 'off-days' or even 'special treats' where we knowingly give him something not on his diet. The price he pays in diarrhea and weird behavior for eating something he can't handle is nowhere near worth the short-term enjoyment of the moment. Plus, saying no 100% of the time is infinitely easier on him (and us) than saying no 99% of the time.

Making Healthy Choices

As he got a little older, Brodie began to identify most of the foods he could and could not eat. At age four, he started reading the ingredient lists and would often say, "This one has milk. Milk is not okay for my tummy." Or, "I think I am going to call the company to see if this jelly is okay." He'd then proceed to pick up the phone and dial some random number!

As Brodie gets older we are hoping it will become easier to give him special treats. These treats could include a larger variety of gluten-free grains and other ingredients that may allow him to enjoy healthier versions of snacks such crackers or a few more types of cakes, cookies, etc.

Consequences of Unhealthy Choices

We do not foresee ever placing Brodie back on gluten or casein. We have heard of some families trying *this and experiencing unfortunate results. While at first, many of them report their children doing well for a few weeks or even months, the child's system can eventually revert back to its previous state, causing multiple problems to reemerge.*

When this happens, the child often regresses in all areas of development, costing several months of valuable time used in making up for the skills lost during this process. This tragedy is something we never want to face, and therefore, we consider at least the GFCF portion of Brodie's diet to be a lifelong endeavor.

Reasons for Joy

Improved Food Tolerance

Around age 3 1/2, about a year into Brodie's special diet (generally consisting of only meats, fruits, veggies, olive oil, eggs, tapioca and garbanzo and fava bean flour), we started adding additional foods in, one at a time. Items such as coconut milk, cream of tartar, and aluminum-free baking powder were used in baking his foods for the first time. After a couple of weeks,

Brodie's digestive tract was still handling these foods without any problems.

We were amazed and thrilled since this meant that milkshakes, smoothies, and more importantly, bread, could reenter his world. Brodie was very excited to finally eat bread since prior to this the only grains he was eating were banana pancakes and a pizza crust (see Appendix A for recipes). Alisha's mother worked through about six recipes before landing on a great loaf of yeast-free bread made only with Brodie's ingredients. We now make it on a weekly basis.

Family & Friends' Support

Throughout the process of changing Brodie's diet, we were fortunate to have the full support of our family, as well as his therapists, who agreed to strictly adhere to the specifics of the GFCF diet. We explained Brodie's eating restrictions to each adult involved in his life, whether at home, school or church. Because Alisha attended therapy with him daily, it was relatively easy to monitor Brodie's food intake at school. At home, we placed forbidden foods in our kitchen out of Brodie's reach so there weren't any accidents. At church, we brought Brodie's snack and had the Sunday-school teachers only give him the food that came with him. Since Brodie's only baby-sitter at the time was one of his primary therapists, we had each of Brodie's environments well covered.

Our moms have been, and continue to be, invaluable in our boys' evolving diet process. While neither of them lives in town, they both make routine trips to Trader Joe's (a supermarket where natural foods are sold) for us since we don't have one nearby. They regularly bring us dried and jarred fruits, coconut milk, banana chips (plantains) and macadamia nuts in large quantities, and have spent countless hours in the kitchen making baked goods to stock up our freezer. Brad's mom has also made many variations of frozen banana treats our kids love for dessert. We are forever grateful for the effort our moms put in on behalf of our family. They have played a huge role in brainstorming creative ways to cook without using any of the long list of foods Brodie has to avoid.

Diet Information Resources

Throughout the process of putting Brodie on a special diet, we were helped tremendously by a number of web-sites, other parents of children on the GFCF diet, Karyn Seroussi's book Unraveling the Mystery of Autism and Pervasive Developmental Disorder, and the GFCF Diet Shopping Guide we purchased at the DAN! Conference. This shopping guide is a MUST have for anyone attempting a GFCF diet. This handbook offers a wealth of information about the diet, various household products, and hundreds of food items. It also includes a cheat sheet the size of a business card listing the various gluten and casein ingredients to avoid. In Appendix B contains a list of resources that have been helpful to us in implementing the diet and many other facets of our battle with autism.

CHAPTER 8 –

STEP 8:
CHOOSING BIOMEDICAL INTERVENTIONS

Note: The treatments and interventions discussed here are based on our personal experiences. We are not doctors nor have we been trained in the medical sciences. Any treatment option should be thoroughly discussed with your child's physician/DAN! doctor to be certain that it is appropriate for your child.

Hormone Injections

*B*rodie had been on the GFCF diet for about two months when we took him to see our DAN! doctor,

Dr. John Green, near Portland, Oregon. While we were there Brodie received an infusion (injecting a beneficial substance into the body) of secretin, a gastrointestinal hormone released naturally by the body. Its purpose is to help neutralize stomach acids and also stimulate the production of other digestive enzymes. Dr. Green shared with us that children with autism can show an improvement in both language and intestinal function within 3-6 weeks after receiving secretin. Sure enough, about four weeks after Brodie's appointment, we noticed a heightened awareness of those around him – he began to notice when someone entered the room – and a significant increase in his use of spontaneous language. The following are two excerpts from our journal during this time documenting Brodie's improvement.

*"**Saturday, November 8th, 2003:** Great day! Brodie wanted everyone to clap when he finished his farm puzzle. Receptive language: found turkey, eggs, corn, and an animal in a learning game. Cognitive: used 'potty card' from the bathroom to get me to open the door so he could throw paper in the trash. Brought*

the 'hug mom' card to get my attention while I was helping Jonah (better than yelling!☺). Spontaneous language: said 'Grandma' clearly and towed her to the living room so he wouldn't be alone watching his video. New words: 'dragon', 'trash', 'down', 'play dough', and several others. Stims – none.

Sunday, November 9th, 2003: *New words are coming quickly. Imitation: 'Brodie', 'tractor', and 'butterfly'. He used words with more syllables the last 3-4 days. Spontaneous language: said "Mama open" today with play dough. Initiated game where we ask him to find all the animals in the rainforest puzzle. Also initiated the 'Itsy Bitsy Spider' song. Took Grandma's hand to make her point to objects in a book. Clapped when he found Papa and Grammy in our living room after his nap. Turned one half of a puzzle 180 degrees to align with the other completed half – good problem solving! Went down two new slides at Hawthorne Park. Showed spontaneous affection for Jonah, Moses (our dog) & Kitty (our cat). Stools have been solid all week. Stims: spinning twice; falling action three times."*

Brodie was also given an infusion of glutathione during that same doctor's visit, another naturally occurring molecule made up of three amino acids and found in most cells in the body. Dr. Greene explained that glutathione is required by the body to maintain a normally functioning immune system. Apparently, high levels of heavy metals, such as mercury, deplete this very important antioxidant which serves to help detoxify the intestinal lining of the gut. Dr. Green also started Brodie on a probiotic, which replaces the good bacteria in the stomach. This can be especially important to take when your child is given antibiotics, as the antibiotics not only wipe out the bad bacteria in the body but also the good bacteria that aid in healthy digestion.

Difficulties with Administering Infusions

While we did notice some improvement in Brodie with these infusions, we ran into difficulties administering them. Brodie was extremely uncooperative during the process so it took about fifteen minutes to complete. He became very upset and broke out in a full-sweat using every muscle he had to get away. The nurses giving the shots were excellent, but we decided that the benefits we were seeing were not worth the traumatic experience at his age. Since Brodie was also improving consistently in all areas we were not as eager to try new things. As many parents of children with autism can attest, it is natural to become motivated to try a new treatment when you've hit a lull or plateau in your child's progress. Conversely, when things seem to be progressing well motivation for trying new treatments can understandably be low.

Dietary Supplements

Over the next couple of years we explored a number of different dietary supplements. Supplements of many kinds are often given to children with autism to aid in rehabilitating their digestive tract and to help facilitate cognitive and social development. Among those we have tried in the past, and some we are still using, are: Sacro B, zinc, DMG, calcium powder, everyday vitamins, vitamin C, cod liver oil, krill oil, N-Acetyl Cysteine, glucosamine and glutamine, B6 & magnesium, B12, Yellow Dock, Ferrasorb, I-throid, and various digestive enzymes, including 'Carb Digest'. There are also many supplements we haven't tried yet, primarily because

Dr. Green has felt that Brodie's stomach should first be stabilized for a longer period of time.

Intestinal Tract Testing

Amongst other things Dr. Green tested Brodie for after a couple of years of treating Brodie's intestinal issues was the Helicobacter pylori (or H. pylori) bacteria.

According to the American Academy of Family Physicians, there is evidence that eliminating these bacteria can help heal the stomach ulcers and reduce the chance of reoccurring bleeding in patients who have gastric ulcers.[17] This discovery has led to a change in how ulcers are treated – from antacids and other symptom-relieving methods to antibiotics.

Brodie had an extremely high level of H. pylori, prompting Dr. Green to treat it with antibiotics to try to prevent him from developing an ulcer. Again, as Dr. Green explains it, the more we can make these kids feel better the more they will be able to learn, relate to others, and overcome the many developmental obstacles they face.

Making Regular Doctor Visits

Over and again, we have seen the value of consulting with Dr. Green every few months regarding Brodie's progress. Parents and DAN! doctors both play a vital role in the process of helping these kids thrive. At different times, we've felt like we really had our arms wrapped around the situation and started doubting the need for a consultation – only to be sent away from Dr. Green's office with our heads spinning from all the new things Dr. Green suggested we consider, or treatments we should try, or tests we should run! These experiences have taught us that working alongside a DAN! doctor is absolutely essential, and it's why many people we know of have flown their children in from out of state just to be seen by one of these specialized doctors. Fortunately, almost every state now has at least one if not several DAN! doctors so families aren't forced to travel so far.[18] However, it can be very difficult to get your health insurance provider to cover treatments and even office visits with DAN! doctors.

Chelation Therapy

One of the most promising, and also most controversial therapies being tried by families is chelation therapy. Some swear by it and have seen amazing results, while others will state that it didn't work for them. Such is the world of autism, which is why we encourage parents to investigate each option to see if it's a good fit for your child.

Having never heard of chelation before, we learned from Dr. Green that it is the process of removing heavy metals from the body using powerful compounds that can be damaging to the system. There are a few different chelators used to remove mercury and other metals. Two of the most common are DMPS and DMSA. DMPS is more potent and can be more effective than DMSA, but has not been rigorously tested in children. These agents can be given orally or intravenously. As with any potential treatment, you should always consult with your DAN! doctor as to which method of chelation, if any, is appropriate for your child.

To test for mercury, an individual is given a challenging agent (the same agents used in chelation) and then a blood or urine test is administered. Giving the challenging agent is essentially a round of chelation as the agent seeks out heavy metals in the body and attaches to these molecules. The body is then able to excrete this "joined" molecule, and a test is given to see which metals were retrieved in the challenge and excreted.

Heavy Metals

Brodie's mercury levels never registered above the normal range. However, the level of tin in his body was one of the highest Dr. Green said he had seen. For this reason, we chose to give chelation a try, intravenously. We gave him two injections, spaced a few months apart. After retesting his metals his tin levels had dropped significantly, and therefore we chose to stop chelation for the time being.

We are not sure how Brodie acquired such high levels of tin in the first place. We've guessed maybe from canned foods, or possibly even drinking water. As a result of finding this out, and at Dr. Green's suggestion, we stopped giving him canned foods and started using filtered water to drink.

It is very possible that Brodie also had a high level of mercury in his system, even though the tests showed otherwise. Mercury can be the most difficult metal to detect and also to remove from the body. When a typical person has experienced a high exposure to mercury, if they are not tested relatively soon afterwards, the mercury is gradually flushed from most of the body with the exception of the central nervous system (CNS). Dr. Green shared with us that for some reason, mercury stays in the organs of the CNS much longer than other parts of the body. Surprisingly, the half-life (time it takes to reduce the level by 50%) of mercury in the CNS can be up to 20 years! It is therefore quite possible that a significant amount of mercury may be present and greatly affecting an individual even if the metals test indicates otherwise.

Dr. Green had mentioned the possibility that mercury may also have been a problem for Brodie. Since tin is easier for the challenging agent to find in the body and attach to, it will cling to the tin molecules and leave the mercury undetected. However, because Brodie was continuing to improve significantly over time, and *due to his extremely fragile gastrointestinal system, we chose to discontinue chelation.*

The controversy surrounding chelation is much like other treatments for autism. Little testing and few studies have been performed for chelation in children. Some in the medical profession question using such strong compounds on children without first having rigorously tested the process.

However, as with many other alternative treatment methods used in the autism community, some of the anecdotal evidence is hard to ignore. Many parents report their child as being "fully recovered" from autism after successful chelation. As a parent, hearing stories like this brings much excitement about the prospect for improvement.

However, these compounds are very strong for young little bodies and in many cases adverse side-effects are reported, including: headaches, nausea or upset stomach, diarrhea, fever, joint pain, skin rashes, and in one nationally publicized case, even death.[19] For this reason, we can't stress enough that it is essential for parents to collaborate closely with their DAN! doctor when making a decision about whether or not to try chelation.

Immunizations

Another controversial decision parents of kids with autism are making is whether or not to immunize their children. Though studies are cited by physicians apparently showing no link between immunizations and autism, there are an overwhelming number of anecdotal stories (i.e. personal testimonies from families) that seem to link the two.

Immunizations & Autism

Though many drug companies have sought to remove mercury from their immunizations, there are many that still contain the heavy metal which is used as both a preservative and a sterilizer. The shot most commonly complained about by some of these families is the 'MMR' shot (Measles-Mumps-Rubella), which until recently contained a substance called 'thimerosal', a natural preservative that is roughly 49.6% mercury by weight. Though thimerosal has been used in vaccines dating back to the 1930's, it is no longer used in the

MMR shot in part because of the recent public outcry against mercury-containing vaccines.[20] *The Food and Drug Administration's website states:*

"At present, all routinely recommended vaccines manufactured for administration to U.S. infants are either thimerosal-free or contain only trace amounts of thimerosal (less than 0.5 micrograms mercury per 0.5 ml dose)." A list of vaccines and their mercury content can be found online at: http://www.fda.gov/ cber/vaccine/thimerosal.htm#t3[21]

The stories of children "turning autistic" within hours or days of receiving their MMR shot are not hard to find in the autism community. For example, one family we heard from tells of how their daughter developed typically for over two years, until receiving the MMR vaccine. Later that evening, she developed a high fever that persisted for a couple of days, at which point she stopped speaking. Ever since this event (now over 10 years ago), she has had autism. Whether or not this was due to mercury in the vaccine, or perhaps just the fact that live viruses were injected into her susceptible system (as some in the autism community suggest), it's impossible to know at the current level of under-standing of autism.

Unfortunately, this family's story is not unique. Are stories like this one grounds for not immunizing our children, or is that an unfounded overreaction? This is a difficult decision for parents – particularly since many of the vaccines have now been substantially purged of mercury (though mercury has not been completely removed from all vaccines). At the very least, the prevalence of these occurrences within the autism community deserves every family's attention and consideration.

There are some very good books on the topic, such as Stephanie Cave's <u>What Your Doctor May Not Tell You About Children's Vaccinations</u>. In this book, a background of immunizations is given, along with an alternate schedule for administering the high number of vaccines now being given to children in the United States. The basic principle of the book, and also the philosophy adopted by many DAN! doctors, is that too many immunizations are now being given to children at too young of an age for their little bodies to handle. Though many appear able to flush the toxins contained in the vaccines (such as mercury) from their systems, *they're finding that a growing number of kids are genetically susceptible to retaining these toxins for longer periods of time, possibly resulting in a wide variety of brain, gastrointestinal, and neurological disorders.*

Doctors' Recommendations

Consequently, DAN! doctors are often recommending that parents of autism hold off for a while on immunizing siblings of children with autism (as opposed to starting right at birth). Once these kids get a little older, the immunizations are phased in one at a time and spaced out several months apart. By doing this, the goal is to give these little bodies the best chance of accepting the vaccine while lowering the risk of causing long-term damage. Obviously, there is also risk involved in not immunizing, as waves of pertussis and some of the other diseases vaccinated for do break out in the U.S. each year.

We want to stress that the decision of whether or not to immunize is a very personal one that each family should make for themselves after consulting with both their pediatrician and their DAN! doctor. No two families' situations are the same, so making an informed and well thought out decision is crucial.

Prescriptions & Over-the-Counter Medications

In general, over-the-counter (OTC) medications can be used to treat common sicknesses provided the dosage requirements for age are carefully followed and you have consulted with your DAN! doctor. However, many of these medicines have gluten and artificial coloring and flavoring in their ingredients. Dye-free and gluten-free formulas are available for OTC drugs, though it is important to consult with your DAN! doctor first to avoid compromising other treatments underway as a part of your child's overall healing process.

CHAPTER 9 –

OUR LIVES TODAY

Reflecting on Brodie's Progress

*O*ne of our goals from the very beginning was for Brodie to be ready to attend a typical classroom by the time he entered Kindergarten. Thankfully, three years ago, he did just that. He had an aide trained in autism (provided by the school district) help him get started each morning for the first 30 minutes, but after that he was on his own. He visited the resource room twice a week in order to work on socialization and following directions. He also met with a speech thera-pist twice a week – once in the classroom and the other time after school.

During his kindergarten year, we were also fortu-nate enough to take Brodie across town for an hour, two afternoons a week, to another elementary school where he joined the 'STAR' program (Strategies for Teaching based-on Autism Research), a small class made up of other high-functioning, first and second grade students on the autism spectrum.[22] This time was used to pre-teach the skills he was struggling with in his kindergarten class. It was also a great oppor-tunity for him to be able to socialize with kids under the supervision of autism experts who helped facilitate situations catered to the students' specific needs.

The following year, for first grade, we moved Brodie across town to join the STAR program full-time. He spent the mornings in a typical first grade classroom, and the afternoons in the STAR class with other first and second grade students on the autism spectrum. Though Brodie was only in this class for the first part of the year due to our move to Uganda, we were very impressed with the program and felt it was a perfect 'boot-camp' for Brodie to hone in on his social skills before moving to Africa.

When we arrived in Africa, Brodie joined the typical first grade class at a nearby international Christian school. Academically, he was above grade level in reading, writing and math, but in the areas of discipline and social skills he still needed some assistance, which Alisha coordinated with the teacher based on the strategies that were used in the STAR classroom.

Currently, Brodie is a happy and energetic eight-year old. Though he is currently a third grader, we placed him in the fourth grade class to keep him challenged academically. Many people remark upon learning of his autism, that they would have never guessed he was any different from other kids his age. He takes piano lessons, loves to swim, and spends every spare chance he gets practicing soccer in the yard. He brings so much joy and fun to our household. His personality is contagious, and watching his brain work or hearing him explain his thought processes at times is downright astonishing.

Brodie's diet remains a major consideration in our lives today. Through much trial and error, we continue to adjust and perfect the types of food he eats, and are always searching for new foods he can tolerate. While starting him on the diet seemed almost unthinkable in the beginning, we never could have known how hard it would really be. Yet the thing that has kept us going has been Brodie's amazing attitude.

We really are in awe of Brodie's perspective on eating. He rarely complains about not being able to eat something, and instead seeks to understand why his body can't handle certain foods. He reads his own labels and is very good at identifying the ingredients he can't tolerate. At church or at school, he'll turn down anything offered to him by accident. When we think of how difficult it must be for him to stay on such a restricted diet, we are so proud of the way he has responded to it. He has taught us a lot about personal discipline and perseverance.

Behavioral discipline remains a big challenge as we struggle as parents to discern Brodie's defiance from his disability. There are times when we'll say his name repeatedly and get no response because he is so engrossed in something else. Generally, he struggles more with children his age or younger, as "childish" actions easily irritate him. We still go through cycles of struggling with Brodie's different behaviors, much more so than a typical child, but as has always been the case with him, if we step back from the immediate situation and look at the bigger picture over several weeks or months, the graph of his overall improvements still slants upwards.

As we've learned all too many times before, autism is a roller-coaster. You take it one hour at a time, one day at a time, and one school year at a time. Brodie has good days and even good weeks, but the bad days and weeks creep back in every now and then. Sometimes it's a diet issue we're battling. Sometimes it's a biomedical issue. Other times, it's just autism. So we continue to focus on winning the journey without worrying about which destination it leads to – that's God's business.

"Don't you know that the Lord is the everlasting God, the Creator of all the earth? He never grows faint or weary. No one can measure the depths of His understanding. He gives power to those who are tired and worn out; He offers strength to the weak. Even youths will become exhausted, and young men will give up. But those who wait on the Lord will find new strength. They will fly high on wings like eagles. They will run

and not grow weary. They will walk and not faint." - Isaiah 40:28b-31

Our family – Brodie (age 8) is on the left, Graysen (age 5) is in the middle and Jonah (age 6) is on the right.

END NOTES

1. *Based on the autism prevalence rate of 2 to 6 per 1,000 Centers for Disease Control and Prevention, 2001 and 2000 U.S. Census figure of 280 million Americans.*

2. *www.cdc.gov/od/oc/media/pressrel/2007/r070208.htm*

3. *www.autism.org/overview.html*

4. *www.autism.org/overview.html*

5. *www.autism.org/overview.html*

6. *www.autism-society.org*

7. *The National Academy of Sciences: <u>Education Children with Autism</u> (2001). http://www.nap.edu/*

8. *http://www.autism.org/si.html*

9. *The National Academy of Sciences: <u>Education Children with Autism</u> (2001). http://www.nap.edu/*

10. *National Research Council (2001) Educating Children with Autism. Committee on Educational Interventions for Children with Autism. Catherine Lord and James P. McGee, eds. Division of Behavioral and Social Sciences*

and Education. Washington, DC: National Academy Press.

11. *Unraveling the Mystery of Autism and Pervasive Developmental Disorder: A Mother's Story of Research and Recovery,* by Karyn Seroussi, Broadway Books, Random House (2002)

12. Lewis, Lisa & K. Seroussi (2003). Autism Network for Dietary Intervention (ANDI)**.** Providing help and support for families using a gluten & casein free diet in the treatment of autism and related developmental disabilities. *http://www.autismndi.com*

13. Reichelt, Karl, PhD, A.M. Knivsberg, PhD., & T Hoien, PhD. (2002). A controlled study of dietary intervention in autistic syndromes. Oslo, Norway: Department of Pediatric Research.

14. Krigsman, Arthur (2002). Preliminary data presented at congressional hearing. http://www.autismndi.com

15. Krigsman, Arthur (2002). Preliminary data presented at congressional hearing. http://www.autismndi.com

16. http://gfcf-diet.talkaboutcuringautism.org

17. American Academy of Family Physicians. www.aafp.org

18. http://www.autismwebsite.com/practitioners/us_lc.htm

19. http://www.pittsburghlive.com/x/pittsburghtrib/s_367277.html

20. http://www.immunizationinfo.org

21. http://www.fda.gov/cber/vaccine/thimerosal.htm#t3

22. www.starautismprogram.com

Appendix A:

Favorite Family Recipes

*B*rodie's diet journey has challenged me in an area where I've always felt somewhat incompetent – cooking! When God blessed us with a family of growing boys, I was a bit frantic in the kitchen. Brodie's emerging dietary needs further complicated things. Slowly but surely and with the help of our two moms, we found a way to eat tasty, healthy meals using very few ingredients. It's our hope that these recipes will help other families too, who are challenged by the dietary needs of autism.

Allergen Information

The recipes included in this book are intended to be free of: gluten, casein, soy, corn, processed sugar, preservatives, artificial flavors and colorings, artificial sugars, peanuts, seeds, and yeast. If you add any of these ingredients into these recipes it will likely change the consistency of whatever you're making. Be sure to be flexible if that's the case and adjust the quantities of what you are using as necessary. These recipes were designed for you to experiment with. Even now, living in Africa for a time with a propane oven, I find myself needing to adjust temperatures and quantities of ingredients often. Also, it's entirely possible that the manufacturers of some of the ingredients listed in these recipes will change their products, so you should always verify the current ingredients of any processed foods used especially if you have life-threatening allergies.

Ingredients

The ingredients used in these recipes are usually found in the nutrition section of your grocery store. If you are having trouble finding a certain item, you can try your nearest health food store or order ingredients *online (see Appendix B for a list of companies to order from). Since we are currently living in Africa we actually have certain ingredients such as flour, baking powder and xanthan gum sent over from the States. Once you find a store that carries what you need you'll find the recipe preparation to be pretty simple.*

Using Different Flours

We use four different types of flour for the recipes in this book – a garbanzo/fava bean flour mix, tapioca flour, coconut flour and Tom Sawyer's gluten-free, diary-free, all-purpose flour. Just recently, I began using the Tom Sawyer all-purpose flour since Brodie's stomach seemed to be tolerating a few more foods (ex. white rice). These are the only types of flour I use at this point. If your child's stomach can handle additional kinds of flour I recommend substituting those in as well. This may take a little experimenting, but it is good for your child's stomach to vary the flours you use. In the past I have found that GFCF (Gluten-free Casein-Free) flour mixes, as well as brown and white rice flours, to be the best substitutes provided that your child's system can handle rice. These GFCF flour mixes often help when

---

you are trying to get breads, cakes, and muffins to rise and hold their shape.

Before using honey:

Please be cautious and check with your family pediatrician before giving your child honey. There are potential health risks associated with children who consume honey before 12 months or so of age. It is possible that using honey in these recipes might not be a option for your child.

BREAD

Yeast-Free Bread Recipe

This bread recipe is one my mom created at a time when we were desperate for a loaf of bread Brodie could eat. It's free of everything but the bare necessities and makes for delicious sandwiches, French toast, or plain toast. Because it stores best in the refrigerator or freezer, we warm it in the toaster or microwave before serving.

Wet ingredients:

- *3 eggs*
- *3 tablespoons extra virgin olive oil*
- *2 cups water*
- *1 tablespoon honey (please check with your family pediatrician before giving your child honey)*

Dry ingredients:

- *2 tablespoons date sugar (I use Aunt Patty's Dry Natural Sweeteners)*
- *2 cups tapioca flour*
- *1 cup Tom Sawyer all-purpose flour (www.glutenfreeflour.com)*
- *1 1/2 tablespoons xanthan gum*
- *1 teaspoon sea salt*
- *1 teaspoon cream of tarter*
- *1 tablespoon baking powder*

Preheat oven to 325°F
Preparation time: 15 mins.
Bake time: 1 hr, 20 mins.
Makes two 8" x 4" loaves

Directions:

Oil and flour two 8"x 4" glass loaf pans. Brush olive oil along insides of pan and coat with tapioca flour by patting the outside of the pans to disperse flour evenly.

In a separate bowl combine wet ingredients with a whisk and set aside. Sift together all dry ingredients. Combine both wet and dry ingredients using a mixer on low or a wooden spoon. Mix ONLY until combined. The bread will rise too quickly and create air bubbles if mixed too vigorously. Bread dough should be a bit lumpy.

Pour bread dough into prepared loaf pans. Run a butter knife through the bread batter and firmly pat the bottom of the pan to eliminate air bubbles. Bake for 1 hr. 20 mins. on middle rack of oven. Bread should look golden brown and test clean in the center with a toothpick when ready. Lay loaf pans on their sides to cool. Store bread in refrigerator or freezer. If kept in the refrigerator, bread will keep for at least a week or so before beginning to crumble a bit.

Alternative: *If your child cannot have Tom Sawyer all-purpose flour you can use 1 cup of garbanzo/fava bean flour instead of 1 cup of Tom Sawyer all-purpose flour. If you want to play with the cooking time you can also make great mini-loaves to slice up for snacks.*

Flat Bread or Pizza Crust

This recipe was adapted from a pizza crust I found in an egg lover's cookbook. It's great for those times when you need bread fast. Brodie loves to put turkey, mustard, lettuce and lemon pepper on toasted flat bread for lunch. Our boys also eat it like toast with jam, or pile seasoned, ground turkey on top with cilantro, lettuce, and avocado to make a taco of sorts. It's also great for dipping in soup or for making very tasty pizza (see recipe).

Main Ingredients:

- *6 eggs*
- *1/4 cup olive oil*
- *1/4 cup water*
- *1 cup Tom Sawyer all-purpose flour (www.glutenfreeflour.com)*

Optional Spices to add:

- *1/2 teaspoon ground oregano*
- *1/2 teaspoon celery salt*
- *1/2 teaspoon garlic salt*
- *1/2 teaspoon fresh basil, chopped (optional)*

Preparation time: 5 mins.

Cook time: 10 mins.

Servings: 8

Portion size: 2 triangular slices

Directions:

In a blender beat together all ingredients until smooth. Pour and spread mixture into a 9" round, non-stick skillet with sloped sides for easy flipping and removal. Cook uncovered over medium heat for about 5 minutes. Flip over with a spatula like a pancake once bottom turns golden brown. If crust starts to split as you flip it, slide it out onto a dinner plate first and then flip it back onto the pan. Cook for another 3-5 minutes until flat bread crust is a light, golden-brown and slightly firm. It should be about 1/2 inch thick. Sprinkle a little more garlic salt, parsley and/or celery salt on top for added flavor or for looks if serving plain.

Prepare as you wish or choose your own seasonings to make different kinds of bread. We have mixed in fresh coconut (pre-toasted in pure maple syrup) or nutmeg and honey to make a sweet-bread of sorts. When making sweet-bread I reduce the flour amount to 1/2 cup to thin the bread a bit. When serving pasta I brush the bread with olive oil and sprinkle rosemary and garlic salt on top.

Alternative: *For thinner crust split the bread batter and cook it separately to yield two, 9" round batches of flat bread.*

BREAKFAST

Spiced Banana Bread

This banana bread tastes great by itself, drizzled with honey, or sprinkled with cinnamon. It also keeps well when packed in school lunches or baked ahead of time and stored in the freezer for upcoming family vacations.

*The steps in this recipe can be a bit tricky, so be sure to read through the directions before you begin.

First Ingredients:
- *1 teaspoon baking soda*
- *1/4 cup coconut milk*

Wet Ingredients:

- *2 eggs*
- *3/4 cup coconut milk*
- *1 teaspoon vanilla (alcohol and sugar-free)*
- *3 ripe bananas mashed*

Dry Ingredients:

- *1 cup date sugar (I use Aunt Patty's Dry Natural Sweeteners)*
- *2 cups Tom Sawyer all-purpose flour (www.glutenfreeflour.com)*
- *1 teaspoon xanthan gum*
- *1/2 teaspoon nutmeg*
- *1/4 teaspoon cinnamon*
- *1/2 teaspoon sea salt*

Preheat oven to 375°F

Preparation time: 15 mins.

Baking time: 25-30 mins.

Servings: makes 4 mini-loaves

Directions:

Whisk together the 1/4 cup coconut milk and baking soda in a small bowl and set aside. Mix remaining wet ingredients in a large bowl using a mixer. Sift together dry ingredients in a separate bowl.

Mix 1/2 of the dry ingredient mixture in with the eggs, 3/4 cup coconut milk, vanilla and mashed bananas. Add in the milk/baking soda mixture. Mix in remaining dry ingredients, blending the entire mixture together. Bake in four small loaf pans coated with olive oil on the middle rack for 25-30 minutes. Serve warm or cool with honey or jam.

Banana Pancakes or Waffles

This recipe makes light and fluffy pancakes or waffles. We often freeze them so breakfast is ready to pull out on school mornings when we're in a rush. This recipe gives the best results when using a pancake griddle or waffle iron. One batch makes approximately 8 waffles or 24 small pancakes.

Wet Ingredients:

- *6 eggs*
- *2 cups water*
- *3 ripe bananas*

Dry Ingredients:

- *2 cups tapioca flour*
- *1 cup Tom Sawyer all-purpose flour (www.glutenfreeflour.com)*
- *1 tablespoon baking powder*

Preheat pancake griddle (or electric waffle iron) to 350°F

Preparation time: 5 mins.

Cooking time: Approx. 20 mins. (using pancake griddle)

Servings: 8

Portion size: 1 waffle or 3 small pancakes

Directions:

Grease waffle iron or pancake griddle with a light coating of olive oil. Mix wet ingredients together in a blender. Add dry ingredients and blend until smooth (adding a couple tablespoons of water if needed to thin the batter). Cook waffles until they are a light, golden brown. For pancakes, flip when bubbles begin to form around edge and top of pancakes.

Banana Pancakes with Coconut Milk

This recipe is a slight variation of the recipe above. If your child can tolerate coconut milk, this may be the recipe of choice. Experiment with the two and see what you think.

Wet Ingredients:

- *2 eggs*
- *1 3/4 cups coconut milk*
- *4 tablespoons olive oil*

- *1 teaspoon vanilla (alcohol and sugar-free)*

Dry Ingredients:

- *4 tablespoons date sugar (I use Aunt Patty's Dry Natural Sweeteners)*
- *1 teaspoon salt*
- *1 3/4 teaspoons baking powder*

Last Ingredients:

- *1 1/2 cups Tom Sawyer all-purpose flour (www.glutenfreeflour.com)*
- *3 ripe bananas*

Preheat pancake griddle (or electric waffle iron) to 350°F

Preparation time: 5 mins.

Cooking time: Approx. 20 mins. (using pancake griddle)

Servings: 8

Portion size: 1 waffle or 3 pancakes

Directions:

Grease waffle iron or pancake griddle. Mix all ingredients with an electric mixer or wooden spoon except flour and bananas. Add flour and bananas in last. If you don't like small banana chunks in pancakes, mash bananas well and mix in sooner to minimize or eliminate chunks. Cook waffles until light, golden brown on bottom. For pancakes, flip when bubbles begin to form around the edge and top of pancakes.

Alternative: *These pancakes/waffles also taste great when using fresh or frozen blueberries/strawberries. Add thawed berries right after pouring batter in the pan and have fun. Smiley faces made with blueberries for a mouth and strawberries for eyes are our boys' favorite.*

French Toast

Making French toast is very simple - a favorite weekend breakfast.

Ingredients:

- *Yeast-free bread (see bread recipe) or prepared pancakes*
- *6 eggs*
- *1 teaspoon cinnamon*
- *1/2 teaspoon pure vanilla extract (alcohol and sugar-free)*

Preheat pancake griddle (or electric waffle iron) to 350°F

Preparation time: 10 mins. (including cooking time)

Servings: 4

Portion size: four slices of French toast using bread or pancakes

Directions:

Mix all ingredients together with whisk in a wide, shallow bowl. Dip bread slices in egg mixture and flip each one briefly to coat both sides. Place coated bread slices in pan or on pancake griddle over medium heat and cook until golden brown on both sides, flipping halfway

---

through. Serve with warm maple syrup, blueberry syrup (see below recipe) or honey.

Note: *I use about ten eggs so I have enough batter for the whole family. I dip all of Brodie's bread first before I prepare the rest of the French toast with wheat bread. I use a separate pan and spatula for Brodie's toast to prevent cross-contaminating his breakfast with gluten.*

Fresh Blueberry Syrup

Ingredients:

- *1/8 cup date sugar (I use Aunt Patty's Dry Natural Sweeteners)*
- *1/2 cup hot water*
- *1/8 cup honey (if okay for your child) or pure maple syrup*
- *1 cup frozen blueberries*

Total preparation time: 5 mins.
Cooking time: Approx. 6-8 mins.

Servings: 6-8

Portion size: Approx. 1/8 cup syrup

Directions:

Grind up frozen blueberries and hot water together in a food processor (I use our 'Magic Bullet'). Pour into saucepan over medium heat, slowly adding honey or maple syrup. Stir frequently for a few minutes. Check taste and add more blended fruit or honey if necessary for desired consistency and flavor. Pour over waffles, pancakes, or French toast. Store syrup in refrigerator.

Date-sugared Donut Holes

My mom created this recipe while visiting our family in Africa. She thought it might be fun to come up with a special treat Brodie had never had. They turned out delicious! Just sweet enough to satisfy your cravings! Hope you enjoy them as much as we do.

Wet ingredients:

- *2 eggs*
- *2 cups water*
- *2 tablespoons honey*

Dry ingredients:

- *2 tablespoons date sugar (I use Aunt Patty's Natural Sweeteners)*
- *1 cup tapioca flour*
- *1 cup Tom Sawyer all-purpose flour (www.glutenfreeflour.com)*
- *2 teaspoons xanthan gum*
- *1 teaspoon vanilla (alcohol and sugar-free)*
- *1 teaspoon cinnamon*
- *1 teaspoon cream of tarter*
- *1 tablespoon baking powder*

Other ingredients:

- *Enough olive oil to fill small skillet 1/2 inch deep*
- *1 small paper lunch bag*

- *Enough date sugar to coat donut holes in paper bag (approx. 1/2 cup)*

Preparation time: 30-40 mins. (cooking time included)
Servings: makes about 3 dozen donut holes

Directions:

Combine wet ingredients in large bowl with whisk and set aside. Sift together all dry ingredients in a separate bowl. Slowly mix together wet and dry ingredients. Pour olive oil into skillet until it is about 1/2 inch deep. Heat the skillet slowly to medium heat. Drop batter into skillet 1 teaspoon at a time and flatten a bit with a spoon.

Donuts should cook slowly. When one side is golden brown, flip and brown the other. Stand them on edge to finish all sides of each donut hole. Transfer donuts one by one from pan to paper bag while still hot. Shake bag in order to coat each donut evenly with date sugar. Cool donuts on a cooking rack and store in a covered container in refrigerator. Re-warm donuts before serving.

DINNER

Homemade Pizza

Pizza is one of Brodie's favorite foods so we were determined to find a tasty substitute. Discovering the flat bread recipe (see "Breads" section) was definitely the ticket. This recipe has served us well, especially at children's birthdays and class parties where pizza is always a popular choice.

Pizza Crust:

- *Use flat bread recipe found in "Breads" section of this cook book. Cook crust ahead of time of you'd like. The crust keeps well in the fridge for several days.*

Pizza Sauce:

- *You will need one 15oz. can GFCF pizza sauce. Remember to check ingredients and call the manufacturer if needed for allergen information.*

Ingredients listed as 'natural flavorings' could contain gluten. You should be able to find GFCF pizza sauce either at your grocery store, a health store, or on the internet. The trick for me has always been finding one without cane sugar.

- *I usually buy tomato sauce containing only tomatoes/salt and sweeten it with about two tablespoons of fresh basil, two tablespoons of fresh parsley, and 1/4 cup of date sugar (or slightly more until sweetness is right). Date sugar also slightly thickens the sauce so that it's just right for pizza. I use about half the sauce and freeze the other half for next time.*

Toppings:

For Hawaiian pizza you will need:

- *Deli turkey or chicken meat fried in about 1/4 cup honey until golden-brown*
- *Crushed fresh pineapple (or canned - check ingredients for allergen information)*

For Vegetarian pizza you will need:

- *GFCF pizza sauce (approximately 4 to 8 oz.)*
- *One green bell pepper sliced thin*
- *4-6 mushrooms*
- *1 onion sliced thin*
- *1/8 cup sliced olives (check for additives)*

Preheat oven to 425°F

Preparation time: 15 mins. (cook pizza crust ahead of time)

Cooking time: Approx. 8-10 mins.

Servings: 8

Portion size: 2 triangular slices

Directions:

Make pizza crust using "Flat Bread" recipe. Evenly disperse pre-mixed sauce and sliced veggies over crust and grill pizza on low-broil (or cook at 425°F using middle rack of oven) until veggies are tender and browned slightly on edges. If using an oven cook pizza for 8-10 minutes. If using a broiler check pizza after 5-7 minutes – *just long enough to grill toppings and warm crust. Using flat bread recipe you can either make one or two 9" round pizzas depending on how thick you like the crust.*

Alternative: *Brodie likes it best when I cook the pizza toppings into the crust. To do this, spread flat bread mixture into pan and wait a couple of minutes. Spread sliced veggies on top. Flip pizza crust when light, golden brown on bottom. Veggies will stay and grill on pan as crust cooks. This keeps toppings from falling off the pizza. When crust and toppings are finished cooking add warmed pizza sauce on last.*

Chicken & Bean Soup

This is the boys' favorite soup recipe. We made it from scratch one day as Brodie helped throw in a bit of this and a bit of that until he said in a matter of fact voice, "It tastes good." We now call him Ratatouille in the kitchen ☺. He likes to serve a slice of flat bread (see recipe)

with the soup for dipping. It makes a great meal, especially with a side of assorted fresh fruit on a rainy day.

Ingredients:

- *1 1/2 lbs. pre-cooked, chicken thigh meat (or white meat)*
- *1/2 cup leeks sliced thin*
- *2 cloves freshly pressed garlic*
- *4 ribs of celery sliced thin*
- *1/2 cup cilantro chopped fine*
- *1/4 teaspoon celery salt*
- *4-5 squirts Tabasco (or 1/4 teaspoon chili powder)*
- *1/2 teaspoon sea salt*
- *1/4 teaspoon pepper*
- *48oz. organic chicken broth*
- *4 cups water*
- *Two 15oz. cans of organic black beans, drained*
- *1 cup coconut milk (optional)*

Preparation time: 20 mins.
Cooking time: Approx. 20-30 mins.
Servings: 8-10
Portion size: one cup of soup

Directions:

Lightly brown about 1 1/2 lbs. of chicken thigh meat until cooked thoroughly. Cut pre-cooked chicken into small soup-size pieces or shred with a fork. Transfer chicken into large soup pan. Sauté leeks and garlic in small skillet and add to browned chicken. Stir in all remaining ingredients and bring soup to a boil. Reduce heat and simmer soup for about 20-30 minutes. Add a couple tablespoons of coconut milk to each bowl just before serving to add creamy flavor if desired.

Alternative: *We make variations of this soup often. It's amazing how many great soups you can make with a little chicken broth, some veggies, and a few spices. Be creative and I think you'll be pleased.*

Split Pea Soup

This thick and creamy soup is very filling. It was created by Brad's mom. It can be prepared ahead of time or taken on road trips as well. It's nice to have recipes that can be kept warm in a thermos. Since there aren't really any easy options for buying Brodie dinner on the road we use recipes like these to provide a tasty meal for the boys.

Ingredients:

- *4 cups vegetable broth*
- *3 carrots diced*
- *1 cup green split peas*
- *1 large, yellow onion diced*
- *1 clove freshly pressed garlic*
- *1/2 teaspoon sea salt*
- *1 tablespoon olive oil*

Preparation time: 20 mins.

Cooking time: 1 to 1 1/4 hours

Servings: 6-8

Portion size: one cup of soup

Directions:

In a medium-sized pot bring vegetable broth to a boil. Add in all remaining ingredients. Reduce heat and simmer with lid ajar. Stir as needed until peas disintegrate. Simmer for 1 to 1 1/4 hours total. If served as leftovers add a few more ounces of veggie broth to thin soup.

Turkey & Bean Chili

As with the split pea and chicken bean soup, this is a great dinner for those days when you need to plan ahead. This recipe can also be cooked on low in a crock pot. I like to prepare it midday on Saturday and have it cooking through the afternoon. Serve with tortilla chips (or sweet potato chips in Brodie's case) and an assortment of fruit. Cantaloupe or Honeydew melon is a great choice.

Ingredients:

- *1 1/2 lbs. cooked turkey or chicken, ground or diced*
- *2 medium, yellow onions chopped*
- *3-4 cloves of freshly pressed garlic*
- *8 cups vegetable or chicken broth*
- *4 ribs celery chopped fine*
- *1 can organic northern beans rinsed*
- *1 can organic black beans rinsed*
- *1 teaspoon chili powder*
- *1/2 teaspoon dry mustard*
- *1/2 teaspoon ground basil (I use fresh basil when I have it)*
- *one small bay leaf*

Preparation time: 20 mins.

Cooking time: 1 hour in pot on stove or on low in crock pot for several hours

Servings: 8

Portion size: one cup of chili

Directions:

In a large pot over medium-high heat, brown turkey or chicken meat until thoroughly cooked. Sauté onions and garlic in small skillet until golden brown and combine with meat in pot. Add all other ingredients. Simmer chili on low for about one hour before serving.

Alternative: *If you like a slightly more Cajun meal add 1 8oz. can of mild, green chilies (check for additives), a few squirts of Tabasco, and/or more chili powder to the pot.*

Homemade French Fries

They tasty fries are great with almost any meal. We serve them with breakfast omelets, hamburgers, soups.....pretty much any time of day! They are quick and easy and can be seasoned however you'd like.

Ingredients:

- *2-4 large potatoes sliced approximately 1/8 to 1/4 inch thick*
- *About 1/4 cup olive oil*
- *sea salt*
- *garlic salt*
- *parsley*

Preheat oven to low broil

Preparation time: 10 mins.

Bake time: Approximately 10-15 mins.

Servings: 4

Portion size: 1/2 of a potato cut in rounds

Directions:

Coat cookie sheet with olive oil and set aside. Wash and slice two large potatoes into rounds like potato chips. Lay slices in rows across greased cookie sheet and brush top of each slice with olive oil. Sprinkle garlic salt over fries and cook on top rack of oven for approximately 8 to 10 minutes. Watch closely until you figure out the perfect cooking time for your oven. Remove fries from oven and flip. Place back in oven for another 1 to 2 minutes depending on desired crispness.

*This recipe can easily be doubled or tripled.

Hash Brown Cubes:

Cut potatoes into cubes about 1/2 inch in diameter and boil in a large pot until pierced easily with a fork. Remove potatoes from pot and transfer to a large nonstick, electric skillet (I use my 'green pan' to avoid using Teflon). Fry cubed potatoes in a coat of brushed olive oil until cubes are golden brown. Serve with omelets or use in 'skillet breakfasts' - add cooked hash browns in with cooked scrambled eggs, sautéed mushrooms, bell peppers, and green onions. In our house of growing boys skillet breakfasts are very popular!

Chicken Shish-kabobs

Kabobs are perfect for summer days served with white or brown rice and fresh fruit or salad. The marinade was something we created based on a neighbor's recipe. We left out some of the ingredients due to diet issues and added some of our own. We like to serve kabobs with steamed rice, fresh fruit and tossed salad.

Kabob Ingredients:

- *2 lbs chicken cubed*
- *3-4 green, red, or yellow bell peppers*
- *20 cherry tomatoes*
- *20 small, whole mushrooms*
- *3-4 red onions sliced into fourths*
- *1 fresh pineapple sliced into triangles*
- *15 skewers for grilling*

Marinade Ingredients:

- *1/4 cup pineapple juice (no added sugar or preservatives)*

- *1/4 cup date sugar (I use Aunt Patty's Natural Sweeteners)*
- *1/2 teaspoon garlic salt*
- *2 tablespoons olive oil*
- *1 teaspoon ginger spice*
- *Add other spices as you wish –experiment with this one!*

*Heat grill or broiler ahead of time

Preparation time: 2-3 hours for marinade
Grill time: Approximately 20-25 mins.
Servings: 8
Portion size: 2 vegetable/meat skewers

Directions:

Combine all marinade ingredients in sealable plastic bag. Add in desired amount of chicken or beef. Marinade meat ahead of time in refrigerator for 2-3 hours. Remove meat, saving leftover marinade in bag. Slide sliced vegetables, meat, and pineapple chunks onto skewers. Brush prepared skewers with remaining marinade. Place skewers on hot grill. Turn skewers halfway through grilling. Brush skewers again with remaining marinade and finish grilling.

*This recipe can easily be doubled or tripled for party events or brought prepared to someone's house for a barbecue, all ready to grill.

DESSERT

Carrot Spice Cake/Muffins

This cake was adapted from a family carrot cake recipe. The added spices really make it tasty. It also goes well with the frosting recipe below.

*Use a blender instead of a mixer for this recipe so that the carrots get pureed, spreading the carrot flavor throughout the cake.

Wet Ingredients:

- *2 eggs*
- *1/2 cup olive oil*
- *1/4 cup honey*
- *1 1/2 cups grated carrots*

Dry Ingredients:

- *1/4 cup date sugar (I use Aunt Patty's Dry Natural Sweeteners)*
- *1/2 cup Tom Sawyer all-purpose flour (www.glutenfreeflour.com)*
- *1/2 cup tapioca flour*
- *1/2 teaspoon cinnamon*
- *1/2 teaspoon pure vanilla extract (alcohol and sugar-free)*
- *1/4 teaspoon ginger*
- *1/4 teaspoon allspice*
- *1/4 teaspoon nutmeg*
- *1 tablespoon baking powder*

Preheat oven to 375°F

Preparation time: 15 mins.

Baking time: 30-35 mins. for cake 20- 22 minutes for muffins

Servings: makes one cake or one dozen muffins

Directions:

Mix together wet ingredients in mixer. Add dry ingredients and blend just until consistency is smooth. For cake, pour mixture into greased 9x13 inch glass pan. Bake on middle rack in oven for 30-35 minutes. For muffins, pour into muffin tins using white cupcake papers (I use white to avoid dye). Bake muffins on the middle rack for 20-22 minutes. Muffins and cake taste great when warmed (if not frosted).

Citrus Garden Cake

This recipe was adapted from a cake recipe my mom found in a sugar-free baking cookbook. It's tangy, full of flavor and keeps well in the refrigerator. Hope you find it refreshing too.

Wet Ingredients:

- *3 eggs*
- *1 cup honey*
- *¾ cup orange juice*
- *4 oz. jar of baby food carrots (check for additives)*
- *¾ cup packed, grated zucchini*
- *¾ cup packed, grated carrots*
- *2 teaspoons pure vanilla extract (alcohol and sugar-free)*

Dry Ingredients:

- *1 1/4 cups tapioca flour*
- *1 1/4 cups coconut flour*
- *1 tablespoon baking powder*

Preheat oven to 350°F
Preparation time: 15 mins.

Baking time: cake: approx. 1 hr. large muffins: approx. 30 mins.

Servings: makes one cake or six oversized muffins

Directions:

Combine wet ingredients in mixer on low. Add in dry ingredients. Mix together. Pour batter into large Bundt pan or Bundt muffin tray coated with olive oil. Bake cake on middle rack in oven for about an hour. Bake muffins on middle rack in oven for about 30 minutes. Remove Bundt cake from pan once cool. For muffins, remove and cool on a cooling rack.

Banana Cake

My mom made this cake for Jonah's third birthday by cutting it and shaping it into a train engine with three cars. She found the idea in an old cookbook and altered the recipe. Cake recipes seem to be the hardest to find since they're generally filled with ingredients Brodie can't have. This cake has been perfect for school

---

birthday parties (as cupcakes) and tastes great with the maple frosting below. It also freezes well (frosting and all). We often have cupcakes stored in the freezer for unexpected school parties.

Wet Ingredients:

- *¾ cup honey*
- *2 1/2 tablespoons pure maple syrup*
- *1 teaspoon pure vanilla extract (alcohol and sugar-free)*
- *2 1/2 medium-sized, ripe bananas mashed*

Dry Ingredients:

- *1/4 cup date sugar (I use Aunt Patty's Dry Natural Sweeteners)*
- *1 cup tapioca flour*
- *1 cup garbanzo and fava bean flour*
- *1/4 teaspoon nutmeg*
- *1/2 teaspoon cinnamon*
- *2 teaspoons of baking powder*

Last Ingredient:

- *2 lightly beaten egg whites*

Preheat oven to 350°F

Preparation time: 15 mins.

Baking time: cake: 30-32 mins.   muffins: 16-18 mins.

Servings: makes one cake or a dozen cupcakes

Directions:

Sift dry ingredients together in large mixing bowl. Set aside. Combine all wet ingredients except egg whites in a mixer on low speed. While mixing, slowly add in dry ingredients. Pour in lightly beaten egg whites last. Mix only until combined. Pour into 13x 9 inch glass pan coated with olive oil. Bake on middle rack in oven for 30-32 minutes. If baking cupcakes, recipe yields about 12 large cupcakes plus 6 mini-cakes baked for 16-18 minutes.

Honey Cake

This dessert turned out to be one of Brodie's favorites. It's a great substitute for cake served at weddings and birthday parties. You can also top it with the vanilla frosting below.

Ingredients:

- *10 egg whites (room temperature)*
- *1 teaspoon cream of tartar*
- *¾ cup honey*
- *1 teaspoon pure vanilla extract (alcohol and sugar-free)*
- *1/2 cup coconut flour*
- *1/2 cup tapioca flour*

Preheat oven to 350°F

Preparation time: 15 mins.

Baking time: 60 minutes

Servings: makes 8-10 slices

Directions:

Beat egg whites in mixer at moderate speed just until frothy. Add cream of tartar and beat egg whites until they hold soft peaks. Gradually beat in honey at high speed until whites are stiff. Gently fold in vanilla and flours 1/4 cup at a time with spoon.

Spoon batter into angel food cake pan (ungreased). Cut through batter with serrated knife to remove air bubbles. Bake on middle rack of oven for 60 minutes or until toothpick pierced in center comes out clean. Turn pan over and cool completely. Run butter knife around inside of pan to loosen cake. Enjoy!

Vanilla Frosting

This frosting can be a bit tricky, but is well worth the trouble. Brad's mom created it. It's light, fluffy, and simply sweet without using processed sugar. Our whole family loves it!

Ingredients:

- *1 cup honey*
- *2 tablespoons water*
- *8 egg whites (at room temperature)*
- *1 teaspoon pure vanilla extract (alcohol and sugar-free)*

Preparation time: 20 mins.

Frosts one cake or one dozen cupcakes

Directions:

Bring honey and water to rolling boil in saucepan. Reduce heat and continue cooking until 242°F using candy thermometer. While honey mixture is cooking beat all egg whites for several minutes until they hold stiff peaks. Egg whites should NOT sit for long.

Drizzle hot honey mixture into stiffly beaten egg whites with mixer on high. Once frosting holds stiff peaks turn to lowest speed and drizzle in vanilla. Do NOT over mix.

Spread frosting over carrot or banana cake storing extra frosting in freezer (doesn't keep more than a day in fridge - begins to separate.

Note: *I try to have a batch of cupcakes frosted in my freezer especially for days when I need a quick treat for a birthday in Brodie's class. Be sure to store the cupcakes in an air tight container.*

Sweet Berry Bars

This was originally a muffin recipe given to us by a cook we met in Africa. We substituted a few of the ingredients and turned them into bars. Brodie especially likes them freshly warmed and served with jam.

Wet ingredients:

- *1 egg*
- *1 cup light coconut milk*
- *1/4 cup olive oil*
- *1/4 cup water*

Dry ingredients:

- *1/4 cup date sugar (I use Aunt Patty's Natural Sweeteners)*
- *2 cups Tom Sawyer all-purpose flour (www.glutenfreeflour.com)*
- *1 teaspoon sea salt*
- *1 tablespoon baking powder*

Last ingredient:

- *1 cup fresh or dried blueberries*

Preheat oven to 350°F

Preparation time: 5 mins.

Baking time: 20-22 mins.

Servings: makes about 12 bars

Directions:

Mix together wet ingredients using whisk in large bowl. Sift together dry ingredients in separate bowl. Combine wet and dry ingredients using wooden spoon. Gently fold in fresh or dried blueberries. Spread batter evenly into greased 9x12" cookie sheet with sides 1" tall. Bake on middle rack in oven for 20-22 minutes.

Macaroons

Brad's mom altered an old recipe to make these delicious macaroons. They turned out to be quick and simple, a perfect recipe for when you're in a hurry. Brodie loves these cookies for school snacks. They're also great for serving with homemade ice cream (in place of ice cream cones).

Ingredients:

- *1 large egg*
- *1 egg white*
- *1 tablespoon date sugar (I use Aunt Patty's Natural Sweeteners)*
- *1 2/3 cups unsweetened coconut, medium-shredded*

- *2 tablespoons honey (or 1 tbs. honey/1 tbs. pure maple syrup)*
- *1/4 teaspoon pure vanilla extract (alcohol and sugar-free)*

Preheat oven to 350°F

Preparation time: 10 mins.

Baking time: 15 mins.

Servings: makes about 16 macaroons

Directions:

Combine all ingredients together using wooden spoon or electric mixer on low speed. Coat rounded measuring spoon (size: 1 tablespoon) with light layer of olive oil. Pack cookie dough firmly into rounded measuring spoon. Release each cookie by flipping measuring spoon over, tapping bottom of spoon with table knife. Macaroon should fall out gently onto cookie sheet. Bake macaroons on middle rack for 15 minutes until light golden brown. Cool cookies on cookie sheet before removing with thin spatula. Cookies will not spread when baking. Entire batch fits on single cookie sheet. One batch yields 16 cookies.

Spiced Sugar Cookies

These cookies are great for special occasions. We make them around holidays using festive cookie cutters. They taste great with cinnamon or date sugar sprinkled on top.

Wet Ingredients:

- *2 eggs*
- *¾ cup extra-virgin olive oil*
- *2 teaspoons pure vanilla extract (alcohol and sugar-free)*

Dry Ingredients:

- *1 cup date sugar (I use Aunt Patty's Dry Natural Sweeteners)*

- *2 cups Tom Sawyer all-purpose flour (www.glutenfreeflour.com)*
- *¾ teaspoon salt*
- *1/2 teaspoon ginger (optional)*
- *1/2 teaspoon nutmeg*
- *2 teaspoons cinnamon (for sprinkling on top)*
- *1 1/2 teaspoons baking powder*

Preheat oven to 375°F

Preparation time: 15 mins.

Baking time: 10-12 mins.

Servings: makes 2 dozen cookies

Directions:

Mix wet ingredients together using blender. Combine wet ingredients from blender with dry ingredients in mixer on moderate speed for 30 seconds. Divide dough into four equal parts. Add water or flour one tablespoon at a time until consistency is right for rolling dough. Roll out dough on floured surface. Use cookie cutters to make desired shapes. Place cookies on lightly greased cookie sheet. Sprinkle cinnamon on top of cookies just before baking if desired. Bake on middle rack in oven for 10-12 minutes. One batch makes approximately 2 dozen cookies.

Hazelnut Cookies

My mom created these moist, delicious cookies. They are designed to be poured and baked in shallow candy molds for special occasions.

Wet Ingredients:

- *2 large eggs*
- *1/2 cup coconut oil*
- *2 large jars of baby food pears: 6 oz. each (check for additives)*
- *1/4 cup honey*
- *2 teaspoons pure vanilla extract (alcohol and sugar-free)*

Dry Ingredients:

- *1/4 cup date sugar (I use Aunt Patty's Dry Natural Sweeteners)*
- *2 cups tapioca flour*
- *1 cup ground unsweetened coconut, medium-shredded*
- *1 cup hazelnuts, ground*
- *1 teaspoon sea salt*
- *2 teaspoons cinnamon*
- *1/4 teaspoon nutmeg*
- *1/4 teaspoon ginger*
- *2 teaspoons baking powder*

Preheat oven to 350°F

Preparation time: 15 mins.

Baking time: 15-17 mins.

Servings: makes about 2 dozen cookies

Directions:

Combine wet ingredients together using mixer on low speed. Add in dry ingredients. Mix all ingredients on medium speed until smooth. Pour batter into large, shallow candy molds or onto cookie sheet brushed with olive oil in desired cookie size. Batter will be slightly runny. Spread cookies out a bit on pan. Shape and size of cookie will make little change during baking. Bake on top rack in oven for 15-17 minutes. One batch makes approximately 2 dozen cookies.

Cookie Clusters

This is a recipe we created in Africa. These cookies take very little time to prepare. Brodie enjoys making them by himself. He's becoming quite the baker these days. Hope you enjoy these healthy treats.

Wet Ingredients:

- *4 large eggs*
- *1/4 cup honey (or 1/8 cup honey combined with one 1/8 cup pure maple syrup)*
- *1 teaspoon pure vanilla extract (alcohol and sugar-free)*

Dry Ingredients:

- *1 cup date sugar (I use Aunt Patty's Dry Natural Sweeteners)*
- *1 1/2 cup ground hazelnuts*
- *4 cups whole grain puffed rice cereal (with no additives)*

Last Ingredients:

- *1 cup granny smith apples thinly sliced (with skin) – optional ingredient*
- *1/2 teaspoon cinnamon*

Preheat oven to 425°F

Preparation time: 10 mins.

Baking time: 10 mins.

Servings: makes 2 dozen cookies

Directions:

Mix wet ingredients together with whisk. Combine wet and dry ingredients with spoon in large bowl until well mixed. Gently fold in apple slices. Spoon batter onto cookie sheet brushed with olive oil in desired cookie size. Spread cookies out a bit on pan. Shape and size of cookie will make little change during baking. Space cookies close together on cookie sheet if you wish. Sprinkle cinnamon over top of cookies just before baking. Bake on middle rack in oven for 10 minutes. One batch makes approximately 2 dozen small cookies.

Alternative: *If your child can't have apples, raisins are a tasty substitute for this recipe.*

Macadamia Nut Cookies

These cookies were derived from a recipe I found in Karyn Seroussi's book, <u>Unraveling the Mysteries of Autism and Pervasive Developmental Disorder</u>. To make them work for Brodie I substituted the sugar and canola oil with honey and coconut oil. This made getting the consistency right a bit difficult. Karyn Seroussi notes these cookies taste much like an English scone. I found they still do even with my alterations. We like to roll them out and use cookie cutters to make special *treats for Christmas and Easter. These cookies also store well in the freezer.*

Wet ingredients:

- *1/4 cup plus 2 tablespoons water*
- *2 tablespoons honey*
- *1/2 cup coconut oil, unrefined*
- *1 teaspoon pure vanilla extract (alcohol and sugar-free)*
- *1 cup macadamia nuts, ground*

Dry ingredients:

- *2 1/4 cups plus 1 tablespoon tapioca flour*
- *¾ teaspoon sea salt*
- *1/2 teaspoon xanthan gum*

Preheat oven to 350°F

Preparation time: 20 mins.

Baking time: 15-17 mins.

Servings: makes 2 dozen cookies

Directions:

Mix wet ingredients together in blender until smooth. Combine with dry ingredients in large bowl. Mix dough thoroughly with wooden spoon. Shape dough with hands into 2 equal balls. Roll cookie dough out on plastic rolling mat or pastry cloth dusted with tapioca flour until dough is 1/4" thick. Add water or flour 1/2 tablespoon at a time if dough is cracking or too sticky. Dip cookie cutters in tapioca flour and press into dough to make shapes. Bake on cookie sheet brushed with olive oil on middle rack in oven for 15-17 minutes. Recipe yields approximately 2 dozen cookies.

Alternative: *Try substituting different types of flour in this recipe depending on your child's dietary allowances.*

Frozen Banana Treats

Brad's mom used to make these sweets for her kids when they were young. They've been a perfect dessert for our family. They're simple to make and great for family functions. A delicious, healthy treat!

Ingredients:

- *4 ripe bananas*
- *frozen or fresh fruit of your choice*

Preparation time: 10 mins.
Freezing time: overnight
Servings: makes 6 popsicles

Directions:

Mash bananas well on chopping block. Spoon mashed bananas into popsicle or candy molds of your choice (ex. we have Winnie the Pooh and large star molds). Slide a wooden popsicle stick into the bottom of each treat. Make a smiley face on each treat using blueberries or raspberries for eyes and strawberries or blueberries for nose and mouth. Freeze popsicles in tray overnight. To release popsicles run hot water over back of pan for 3-4 seconds. Lift popsicles and store each one in a plastic sandwich baggie. Place baggies in large Ziploc or air tight container in freezer. Each batch makes approximately 6 large treats.

Milkshakes, Fruit Smoothies, or Ice Cream

Our boys love this simple recipe! We serve this dessert as milkshakes or ice cream. We make them often since Brodie can eat the same dessert everyone else is having- despite his food intolerances.

Ingredients:

- *1 can coconut milk, chilled is best*
- *1/4 cup honey*
- *3 bananas*
- *1 cup of frozen or fresh fruit of your choice*
- *1 tray of ice cubes (12 large cubes of ice)*

Preparation time: 10 mins.
Mixing time: Milkshakes/smoothies: 3 mins. Ice cream: approx. 25 mins. to freeze

Servings: 6

Portion size: 2/3 cup ice cream OR 1 milkshake/ smoothie (8oz.)

Directions:

Mix all ingredients together in blender until smooth. Blueberries, raspberries, mango, pineapple or straw-berries are great choices. Check for hidden ingredients in your store-bought frozen fruits (sugar is often an additive). Add more honey for desired sweetness.

For morning fruit smoothies rather than milkshakes, leave out ice and replace with water. For ice cream, leave out ice but do NOT add water. Pour blended smoothie mixture into ice cream maker. I recommend investing in a "Cuisinart: Frozen Yogurt – Ice Cream & Sorbet Maker." Cuisinart comes with two bowls. Store bowls in freezer so they're ready to use. Ice cream takes about 20-25 minutes to freeze. Leftovers can be poured into plastic, upright popsicle molds to eat later.

Notes:

We make smoothies so often that I always store coconut milk in the refrigerator. Then I'm sure it's ready when I need it.

Plastic, upright popsicle molds are different than candy tray molds. Smoothie mixture above is too runny for freezing in flat, candy tray molds.

* *Finished ice cream is still smooth enough to fold in raspberries or blueberries if you wish. We also add pure vanilla extract to our milkshakes. As you've probably guessed, you really can't mess up this recipe.* ☺

Alternative: *My favorite treat is peppermint ice cream (using no ice). Make blended ice cream mixture using only bananas for fruit. Add* **ONE** *drop of pure peppermint oil (found at health store – check for hidden ingredients). Around Christmas time we make peppermint ice cream and decorate it with pomegranate pieces and a mint leaf at the top.*

Alternative: *If you want to make an "Orange Julius" of sorts try using:*

- *1 can coconut milk, chilled is best*
- *1 cup pure orange juice (check for additives)*
- *3 bananas*
- *1 tray of ice cubes (12 cubes of ice)*

A final note:

I really hope you enjoy these recipes and find them helpful for feeding your family. I also hope you find ways to vary these creations and tailor them to fit your own dietary needs. Think out of the box; substitute ingredients. You'll be amazed at what you come up with.

Appendix B:

Resources

*T*he purpose of this book is to give parents a way to get educated on the basics of autism quickly so they can get started helping their child as soon as possible. Consequently, we omitted a lot of in-depth information in order to keep the book short. However, once the process is underway, learning more about autism is essential to tackling the disorder long-term. The following list of resources has been very helpful to us during our journey, so we're passing them on. There have been many, many books written on the subject that have good information in them. This list only contains the ones we have read or referenced.

Just because a book isn't on this list doesn't mean it's not worth reading, it's just that we haven't read it yet.

Books

<u>*Unraveling the Mystery of Autism and Pervasive Developmental Disorder: A Mother's Story of Research and Recovery*</u>
Author: Karyn Seroussi
Broadway Books, Random House (2002)

<u>*Let Me Hear Your Voice: A Family's Triumph Over Autism*</u>
Author: Catherine Maurice
Ballantine Books, Random House (1993)

<u>*Overcoming Autism: Finding the Answers, Strategies, and Hope That Can Transform a Child's Life*</u>
Author: Lynn Kern Koegel, Ph.D. and Claire LaZebnik
Penguin Group (2004)

Treating Autism: Parent Stories of Hope and Success
Edited by: Stephen M. Edelson, Ph.D. and Bernard
Rimland Ph.D.
Autism Research Institute (2003)

Recovering Autistic Children
Edited by: Stephen M. Edelson, Ph.D. and Bernard
Rimland Ph.D.
Autism Research Institute (2006)

Special Diets for Special Kids: Understand and
Implementing Special Diets to Aid in the Treatment of
Autism and Related Developmental Disorders
Author: Lisa Lewis, Ph.D.
Future Horizons Inc. (1998)
Edited by: Judy DeHart
You can order this guide through the GFCF Diet
Support Group: http://stewartdehart.stores.yahoo.net/
noname1.html

Helpful Websites

ASA- Autism Society of America – improving the lives of all affected by autism
www.autism-society.org

ARI- Autism Research Institute
www.autism.com

Center for the Study of Autism

Generation Rescue
www.generationrescue.org

Helicobacter pylori Treatment
www.aafp.org/afp/20070201/351.html

Hidden Recovery
www.hiddenrecovery.com

List of vaccines and their mercury content
www.fda.gov/cber/vaccine/thimerosal.htm#t3

Strategies for Teaching based-on Autism Research
www.starautismprogram.com

TACA – Talk About Curing Autism
www.talkaboutcuringautism.org

Treating Autism: Because Autism IS Treatable
www.treatingautism.ik.com/links/all.ikml

Treatment Options for Mercury/Metal Toxicity in Autism and Related Developmental Disabilities: Consensus Position Paper- Autism Research Institute www.autism website.com/ARI/dan/heavymetals.pdf

Websites for Gluten-free, Casein-free Shopping

Gluten Free Mall
http://www.glutenfreemall.com/

Kirkman – A great resource for finding supplements that fit your child's dietary needs
www.kirkmanlabs.com

Autism Web – A Parent's Guide to Autism and Pervasive Developmental Disorder (PDD)
www.autismweb.com/diet.htm

The GFCF Diet Support Group (2003)
www.gfcfdiet.com

Enjoy Life
www.enjoylifefoods.com

Tom Sawyer Gluten Free Products
www.glutenfreeflour.com

www.kinnikinnick.com

Miss Roben's Mixes
www.allergygrocer.com

Appendix C:

Sample Charts & Behavior Tracking

Chart C.1a: Brodie's Sleep Patterns: Week of Oct. 27th - Oct. 31th, 2003						
Shortly after this time, Brad and I decided to do away with Brodie's afternoon nap. This was a huge turning point for us. While Brodie still struggled with sleeping through the night, he at least fell asleep easily around 7:30 pm. rather than a couple of hours later, allowing Brad and I to enjoy our evenings together.						
	Naptime Sleep Pattern			Nighttime Sleep Pattern		
	Trouble falling asleep?	# of Hours Slept	Woke up on his own?	Trouble falling asleep?	# of Hours Slept	Woke up following morning on his own?
Monday	no	2 1/2 hr.	no	no	7 hr. 45 min.	yes, 5:30 am
Tuesday	no, 12:00 pm	2 hr. 10 min.	yes	no	8 hr. 45 min.	yes
Wednesday	no	3 hr.	no	no	9 hr.	yes
Thursday	no	2 hr 20 min.	no	no	9 1/2 hr.	yes
Friday	took 30 min.	2 1/2 hr.	no	no	9 hr. 15 min.	yes
Saturday	took 30 min.	2 hr. 10 min.	no	no	9 hr.	yes
Sunday	no nap, tried for 40 min.	slept 1 hr. at store	no	no	9:30pm - 2am 4:30am - 8am	no

Chart C.1b: Brodie's Stool Patterns: week of Oct. 27th thru Oct. 31th						
	Time #1	Consistency	Time #2	Consistency	Time #3	Consistency
Monday	after nap	diarrhea, large amt.	after dinner	diarrhea/undi-gested food		
Tuesday	before breakfast	trace amt. of diarrhea	4:00pm	diarrhea, foul smell	6:00pm	diarrhea, foul smell
Wednesday	11:00am	sm. amt., solid	11:00am	diarrhea, in diaper	after dinner	diarrhea/undi-gested food
Thursday	after dinner	large amt., solid sects.				
Friday	none					
Saturday	after breakfast	sm. amt., solid	11:00am	soft, in diaper	after lunch	std. in diaper, lots, soft
Sunday	after lunch	solid, normal	after dinner	std. in diaper, soft, normal		

Chart C.2: Changes in Behavior: Week of Oct. 13th thru Oct. 19th, 2003

MONDAY	Eye contact was about a 3 today. Hard to get Brodie's attention today. Several time-outs for not coming. Seemed more hyperactive than last couple of days. Tried hitting me (lightly) several times today to get my attention and threw several things on the floor while eating. Seemed to be testing the limits as he looked for my reaction. Therapists also seemed to struggle to get his attention. Flitzed from one activity to another (even with puzzles), not wanting to finish tasks. In his bath, scratched at his right buttock a lot (possible yeast overgrowth?).
TUESDAY	Eye contact was about a 4 today. Focused well during one on one time with both speech therapist and autism consultant today. Expressive language during speech was great. Had trouble coming when called again today and tried hitting me three times (hit Brad once, lightly). Still seemed easily distracted today and very tired tonight - because of long nap? Did not appreciate the appearance of frozen green beans. Sensory: Brodie played in the sand box today. Willingness to dig in sand improved throughout.
WEDNESDAY	At school the therapists rated Brodie's eye contact a 4 out of 5. Seemed a little tired but did very well with expressive language and PECS requesting during one on one time. Enjoyed both the bolster and platform swing and tolerated sifting through popcorn foam to find balls. Sat at the bar and played with play dough (with gloves on!) and markers with me for 45 mins. Great attention span. Seemed happy and energetic too. No stims today that I saw, except for fingers in his mouth twice.
THURSDAY	Eye contact again today was about a 4. Shook his head back and forth for a short period while in the baby back pack. Also held his hand in his mouth on the way home and scratched at his buttocks while taking afternoon bath with epsom salt. Scratched both buttocks during night bath. *Ask Dr. Green about yeast at net appointment.
FRIDAY	Eye contact was about a 3 today. Woke up at 4:45am. Stayed in bed until 6:15am. Reasons for waking early: I put a blue fizzy color ball in the afternoon bath with epsom salt and realized that I had done after about 1/2 had already dissolved. Also had tortilla chips - take out corn! Think it's causing irritability and restlessness. Good eye contact and expressive language at school - hyperactivity level tonight. Did great tonight at the soccer field after having a 2 1/2 hr. nap. Used the hug mom PECS card for first time on his own (requesting a hug). Didn't need to be introduced to it - just ran it to me. :)
SATURDAY	Eye contact was about a 4 today. Brodie was a great listener today at the soccer field. Had a lot of trouble going down for a nap (took an hour). Hyperactivity level normal. After dinner had explosive diarrhea twice. Would yell just before and then race for his card and not make it in time. Poor guy. Tried to put my finger into his mouth. Not sure if it was his tongue or gums that were hurting. Great expressive language tonight (ex. said "puzzle" very clearly.)
SUNDAY	Eye contact was a 4 today. Went to church this morning. Brodie was in a new room. I went with him. He explored it gleefully, climbed through the tunnels, and played with the toys but didn't seem interested in what the other children were doing. On our way to Portland for Brodie's appt. with Dr. Green, our car broke down. Brodie did great through it all. He has also learned how to play the " Hello, do you like my hat game" which we derived from the Dr. Seuss book Go, Dog, Go! (his favorite).

Chart C.3a: Brodie's Food Intake: Week of Dec. 8th thru 14th, 2003

At the time this chart was created we were experimenting with different gluten-free, casein-free foods. Brodie had started the GFCF diet, but finding a wide variety of healthy foods that were compatible with Brodie's stomach (that he would eat willingly) was a struggle. This was just the beginning for Brodie. His diet changed drastically in the coming years. He now loves and is able to eat meats, fruits and vegetables that work well for his body.

	Mon	Tues	Weds	Thurs	Fri	Sat	Sun
Breakfast	waffle w/ map. sryp, banana, applesauce w/ new probio & sacro B, & DMG w/ juice	waffle w/ map. sryp, banana, applesauce w/ new probio & sacro B, & DMG w/ juice	waffle w/ map. sryp, applesauce w/ new probio & sacro B, & DMG w/ juice	waffle w/ map. sryp, applesauce w/ new probio & sacro B, & DMG w/ juice	waffle w/ map. sryp, applesauce w/ new probio & sacro B, & DMG w/ juice	waffle w/ map. sryp, applesauce w/ new probio & sacro B, & DMG w/ juice	waffle w/ map. sryp, applesauce w/ new probio & sacro B, & DMG w/ juice
Morning Snack	1/3 cheetah bar, ham slices w/ mayo & must, chips, pineappple, fruit strip, water	chips, 1/2 cheetah bar, fruit strip, water	soy yogurt, fruit strip, pineapple chunks, water	pineapple chunks, 2/3 cheetah bar, kettle chips, green DD lollipop, water	couple bites yogurt, couple chips, fruit strip, 1/4 banana, water	pineapple, rice crackers, fruit strip, water	3/4 fuji apple, fruit strip, rice chex, kettle chips, water
Lunch	soy yogurt, carrots, water	ham sand w/ mayo & must, blueberries, one apple slice, rice chex. water	hotdog w/ ketchup, chips, couple carrots, 2/3 banana, water	ham sand w/ mayo & must, chips, apple fruit leather, water	red dumdum lollipop from Brad. McD's french fries, ham sand w/ mayo & must, sm amt yogurt, water	ham slices w/ mayo & must, kettle chips, few carrots, yogurt, water	ham cubes w/ mayo & must, soy yogurt, hotdog w/ ketchup, red dumdum lollipop, soy ice cream, water

Chart C.3b: Brodie's Food Intake: Week of Dec. 8th thru 14th, 2003							
	Mon	Tues	Weds	Thurs	Fri	Sat	Sun
Dinner	refused classico spagetti sauce, mushrooms & rice noodles. Ate hot dogs, peas & carrots, water	hotdogs w/ ketchup & must, peas & carrots, 1/2 banana, baked steak fries. DMG w/ grape juice	hotdogs (1/2 Beeler's dogs) w/ ketchup, steamed carrots & grn beans wl brn sug, steak fries. DMG w/ water	refused yogurt, applesauce, & turkey. Ate green beans & carrots, hotdog w/ ketch, toast w/ jam, water	ham cubes, few carrots, rest of McD's fries. Did not finish ham so no ice cream, water	2 hot dogs w/ ketchup, green beans, baked fries, 3/4 tropical fruit cup. DMG w/ juice	McD's hamb & french fries w/ ketchup, green beans, DMG w/ water
Evening Snack/ Dessert	soy ice cream w/ choc syrup, applesauce w/ cust. probio, DMG w/ water	apple lolli to wake him up b4 dinner, soy ice cream w/ choc syrp, 4oz rice milk bottle	butterscotch lollipop, 3/4 banana. 1 bite applesauce w/ cust probio. Pacific rice milk (only drank 1oz)	soy ice cream w/ choc syrp, no DMG or probio tonight (forgot), 4oz pacific rice milk bottle	fruit strip at Costco, rice chex , applesauce with cust. probio. DMG w/ juice at dinner, 1/4 banana. 4oz rice milk bottle	fruit strip (2) 2 tblsp. ice cream w/ cust. probio. 4 oz rice milk bottle	rice crackers, one bite applesauce w/ cust. probio, 4 oz rice milk bottle

Chart C.4: Brodie's Daily Schedule

The following is an example of Brodie's daily schedule when he was around 20 months old – about three months after we discovered his autism. You will only find one formal therapy session within this schedule since Brodie was only being seen a couple of times a week. At this point we were doing most all the therapy ourselves while we waited for his first formal IFSP (Individualized Family Service Plan) meeting. This schedule was written for Brad's mom and dad, who were watching Brodie for the day while we traveled north for a medical appointment for our other son Jonah.

6:30 or 7:00am- Brodie wakes up
(sometimes earlier)

- *Play (ex. puzzles, stacking blocks) for 15 minutes with Brodie before getting him dressed.*

7:30am- Play time

- *Work with Brodie on simple commands such as open, shut, my turn, your turn, help, and look. We usually play in the family room for this portion.*

8:00 or 8:30am- Breakfast Routine

- *Eat*
- *Brush teeth (Singing "Row, Row, Row Your Boat").*
- *Play time with toys (again working on commands) - in Brodie's room this time for a change of scenery.*

10:00 or 10:30am- Errands *- I usually run one or two errands with Brodie each morning. He really likes to get out of the house for awhile - and I don't want him to lose his desire for going places. We use errands as a time for practicing:*

- *Pointing at things we see in the store*
- *Naming different items as we add them to our shopping cart.*

11:30am or 12:00pm- Lunch

- *If Brodie looks tired enough to fall asleep on the way home from errands then I usually bring lunch with us and we have a picnic somewhere. ☺ He is pretty good at being transferred from the car to his bed as long as he hasn't been asleep for more than 15 minutes or so. If we eat lunch at home I play with Brodie for half an hour or so after lunch and then take him on a neighborhood walk in the stroller. He has been having a horrible time going down for naps, but usually falls asleep in the stroller on our walk. He can be transferred to his bed from there as well.*

12:30 or 1:00pm- Naptime

- *Brodie should sleep anywhere from 1 1/2 to 2 hours.*

2:00 to 3:00pm- Brodie wakes up - Snack time

- *Brodie will want a bottle (3/4 water, 1/4 juice,) and for you to read a few books to him.*

  *At different points in the book I randomly stop reading and wait for Brodie to look up at me. Once he does I take that as my cue to continue reading. Brodie also likes to swing in the backyard (a perfect opportunity for teaching, "Ready, set, go!") I let him swing for about 15 – 20 seconds, then stop and say, "Ready, set… and wait for him to attempt the

word "Go!" When he mutters even a sound, whether correct or not, I start swinging him again to reward him. In the afternoons we also work with puzzles, crayons, blocks, etc.

- *We usually go on a walk with the stroller after nap if we haven't gone earlier. Walks are great for pointing things out like airplanes, cars, dogs, houses, etc.*
- *ON MONDAYS Brodie has play/speech therapy in our home at 3:20pm for one hour.*

5:30 or 6:00pm-Dinner

- *While I make dinner Brodie often gets to watch a Veggie Tales, Baby Bumblebee, or Baby Einstein video. Brad is usually with him during the video. Brad will pause Brodie's movie multiple times to interact with him by saying things like, "Look, I see Larry." Brodie knows he has to make eye contact if he wants the video to continue.*

A couple of Brodie's favorite activities:

- *Vacuuming. Brodie really just wants to turn the vacuum off and on repeatedly. So, we use this as an opportunity for eye contact since he REALLY wants you to move your hand off the switch, but knows you won't until he looks at your eyes.*

- *A walk without the stroller (while he works on holding hands and one-step commands: "Stop" and "Go")*

- *More puzzles. Brodie will do puzzles for hours if you let him. Puzzles are a great pre-bath activity since they are also calming for him.*

7:30 or 8:00pm- Bath time

- *Brodie now understands the phrase, "Do you want to take a bath?" and will tow you there by the hand. When he gets there, he needs to throw the little green frog in the tub. Then you can turn on the water. He will also need to help you take off his shirt, etc. (we are working on his adaptive skills).*

Brodie also loves the shower head on his back and will want to stand up while you rinse his hair with the cup (he gets scared if he is sitting down).

- *After bath Brodie likes to sit on the couch with Brad and drink a bottle of rice milk at about 8:30 or 9:00. When he is finished I brush his teeth.*

Between 8:45 and 9:15pm- Bed time
- *Before bed, one of us prays with Brodie and then puts him in bed and sings him a song. The yellow blanket is his indication that it is time for bed. I usually bring it to him and tell him it is time for ni-night.*

A Couple Reminders:

- *During play-time: If Brodie is playing with something and brings it to you, he probably needs help. Don't give him any until he makes eye contact.*

Just wait for it silently and if needed prompt him with, "Look." When

he does, say, "Oh, you want help?" and then proceed.

- *When Brodie tows you somewhere or wants you to pick him up he needs to make eye contact first.*

- *Brodie seems to understand the following phrases:*

Brodie do it

Brodie help

Put away

Come see me

Finished

All done

Push and Pull

Open and shut

Do you want help?

Do you want a bath?

If you are finished, give it to me (I use this with food so it doesn't end up on the floor).

Time-outs:

Brodie understands what a time out is but will try to flop over or get up in the middle. I usually stay with him for learning purposes. He may need your help sitting still. As soon as he is still I usually say, "Okay Brodie, come say sorry." His sorry is a hug. Then I tell him again what he CAN do, or NEEDS to do (ex. "Brodie, do gentle to Kitty"). He has been struggling with time outs so they are very short and used only after I have given him a warning.

Chart C.5: Sample Kindergarten Schedule

Below you will find an example of a schedule I made for Wednesdays when Brodie was in Kindergarten. He was getting stressed about each day's schedule, so I made one for each day of the week, ran off a bunch of copies, and laid the next day's schedule out on the kitchen counter the night before so that he could find it first thing in the morning. Having his own schedule he could refer to (since he could read at that point) any time of day during the week took a lot of stress off of Brodie. To this day he loves to know what's on the schedule first thing in the morning. When the schedule changes as the day wears on, and it often does, we practice being flexible – another great learning opportunity.

Note: There are no times on this schedule because at this point in Brodie's life seeing exact times made him more stressed. He really just wanted to know what was coming up next. When the time comes, it will be your job to decide what your child's schedule should look like to fit his or her own needs.

Wednesday Schedule:

- *Get Dressed*
- *Eat Breakfast*
- *Brush teeth and comb hair*
- *Kindergarten- then home again*
- *15 minutes of free choice time*
- *Snack*
- *Rest time and naps for boys (Brodie: silent reading and homework time)*
- *Eat lunch*
- *Indoor swimming*
- *Short errand*
- *Play at home*
- *Video*
- *Dinner*
- *Bath, brush teeth & put on jammies*
- *Family time: books, puzzles and games*
- *Pray*
- *Bedtime for the boys*

LaVergne, TN USA
19 February 2010
173679LV00001B/38/P